Unfolding *the* Heart

Unfolding *the* Heart

One Woman's Quest for True Nature

ROSANNE ANNONI

SWP

SHE WRITES PRESS

HUMAN AUTHORED Reg #2174546

Published in 2026 by
She Writes Press, an imprint of The Stable Book Group

1569 Solano Ave #546
Berkeley, CA 94707
https://shewritespress.com
Library of Congress Control Number: 2026907240
ISBN: 979-8-89636-152-7
eISBN: 979-8-89636-153-4

Interior Designer: Andrea Reider

Printed in the United States

Names and identifying characteristics have been changed to protect the privacy of certain individuals.

For Michael H. Ward

July 1, 1944–July 30, 2020

Always here

My advice to you is not to undertake the spiritual path. It is too difficult, too long, and too demanding. It is really going to ask everything of you. So, it is best not to begin. However, if you do begin, it is best to finish.

—Chogyam Trungpa

Prologue

1956

Every classroom at St. Catherine of Siena in Allentown, Pennsylvania, looked the same: rows of wooden desks facing a chalkboard across the front wall. Above the chalkboard hung a cross with a dying Jesus, streaks of blood trickling down his face from a crown of thorns.

I was in love with my fifth-grade teacher, Sister Emily Joseph. She was young, with cobalt blue eyes and freckles that dotted her peachy-skinned face. Though her coif and veil covered her head, I was certain that she had flaming red hair. I raised my hand a lot, to answer questions or volunteer to erase the chalkboard, but the closest I got to Sister was at recess. Sometimes she'd swing the jump ropes or play ball with us, hiking her full-length habit to just above her ankles, the long black rosary that hung from her belt flying in the air. Her smell was intoxicating, the sweetness of talcum powder mixed with yards of musky black wool serge.

One afternoon, while I was staring at the cross above Sister's head, Jesus opened his eyes and looked right at me. The classroom flooded with light. Objects and people disappeared, even Sister Emily Joseph. I stared in awe. His mouth moved slightly as he called me to become a nun. Warmth filled my chest, and I silently thanked him for choosing me to be his bride. That's what nuns were called back then, Brides of Christ, because of their total commitment to God.

Up until that moment, I had never imagined becoming a nun. I continued to stare at the cross until Jesus turned back into a statue. Sister Emily Joseph was writing something on the chalkboard. None of the other kids seemed to notice what had happened, and I didn't dare interrupt Sister in the middle of a lesson to tell her.

Instead, I put my hand on my chest, which still felt warm, and vowed to devote my life to serving God.

"Mom, Mom!" I shouted as I ran into the kitchen, my bookbag still slung over my shoulder. "Jesus talked to me today! He told me he wants me to become a nun, just like Sister Emily Joseph."

Mom had her back to me as she stirred meat sauce on the stove.

She turned slowly, moving the wooden spoon dripping with sauce into her left hand. I was sure she was getting ready to hug me.

Thwack! Her right hand caught me square on the side of my face, throwing me off balance.

"*Don't you ever say that again.* Do you understand me, Rosanne?" She glared at me through narrowed eyes, her lips disappearing into a thin line.

Trying to find my footing, I stared at the floor, which had splotches of what looked like blood. But when I reached up to touch my face, it was hot and dry. In a daze I walked upstairs, crawled into my bed, and lay on my back, hands folded across my chest. I stared at the ceiling, not moving a muscle.

2006

Huge pine and birch trees surrounded Pema Chodron's rustic cabin, set down and back from Gampo Abbey's main dirt road. A narrow walkway covered with a few inches of snow led to the front door. When I opened it, I was greeted with a blast of hot air and felt a wave of relief. I wouldn't have to worry about being cold inside my cabin.

I hadn't become a nun, but here I was, staying in a nun's home for the next four weeks. Not the kind of nun my mother had pictured, and not the kind of spiritual apex I had imagined as a ten-year-old girl.

The walls of the cabin were lined with photos of Pema's spiritual teachers. Her first, the famous Chogyam Trungpa, is credited with bringing the Tibetan teachings to America. He fled Tibet in 1957 along with the Dalai Lama and died in 1987. He looked young in the photo, pitch black hair, an impish smile, and intense eyes that followed me wherever I stood in the room. Just inside the door of the main bedroom hung a life-size photo of Trungpa's son, Sakyong Mipham, who took over as the head of the Shambhala organization when his father died and at that time was Pema's teacher. Unlike his father, Sakyong was strikingly tall and handsome with an open, smiling face.

I had read a few of Trungpa's books but was put off by stories of his alcoholism and fierce approach to practice. It felt strange to be suddenly immersed in his world, and I wondered if I might have a change of heart about him during my stay. A small twin-size bed was set into the corner of the bedroom, with a desk next to it under a picture window framing the woods. I imagined myself sitting there each morning, drinking tea from my new teacup—a red teacup that I had ceremoniously unwrapped and placed on the kitchen counter before I even unpacked my clothes and supplies.

It sat, waiting, in the kitchen down the hall, past a tiny bathroom and a second bedroom that doubled as a meditation room. It was the only splash of color in the otherwise neutral space.

PART I
Turning Inward

God speaks to each of us as he makes us,
then walks with us silently out of the night.

You, sent beyond your recall,
go to the limits of your longing.
Embody me.

Let everything happen to you: beauty and terror.
Just keep going. No feeling is final.
Don't let yourself lose me.

Nearby is the country they call life.
You will know it by its seriousness.

Give me your hand.

—Rainer Maria Rilke,
Book of Hours: Love Poems to God

CHAPTER ONE

Traveling to the End of the Earth

I'd gotten that red teacup just days before arriving at Gampo Abbey, after a van had dropped me off at my hotel in Halifax the night before my long drive to the abbey. With just an hour left of daylight, I bundled up in my newly purchased chocolate brown L.L.Bean ultrawarm down coat, which was just long enough to cover the tops of my Ugg boots. With my coat zipped to my chin, I pulled a shearling hat over my ears and set out for a short walk along the main road.

A charming teashop, the only store still open, lured the inveterate shopper in me. *One last spree before dissolving into emptiness!* I'd already shipped a large box of supplies to the abbey: my favorite chai and black tea blend, packets of protein powder, organic nuts, gluten free oatmeal and crackers, vitamins, and herbal remedies from my acupuncturist.

Crossing the shop threshold, I scanned the contents of the shelves. An inner voice chided me. *You've already shipped enough supplies for a year. What more could you possibly need?* Teapots and cups crowded the shelves, along with homemade jams and other delicacies, tempting to someone about to spend four weeks foraging for food from cold storage in the bowels of an abbey. What did I *need*? The answer jumped off the shelf and into my hands: a bright red porcelain teacup with a matching pot nestled on top. Running a hand over the cup's clean lines and smooth surface, my finger curled perfectly around the handle while my other hand easily cradled the cup. I took the cup and pot apart and put them back together a few times, admiring their seamless fit. How ingenious! Of all the similar matching cups and pots, none was as glorious as the red one in my hands.

Walking briskly in the setting sun, I arrived back at the hotel just in time for dinner. It took a few moments for my eyes to adjust to the small, dimly lit dining room. In the dark quiet, I began to feel the first inklings of the solitude awaiting me. I savored each bite of lamb, knowing it was the last meat I would taste for a month. And I ordered dessert, a crème brûlée topped with burnt caramel.

The next morning, with the teacup and pot stuffed into my shoulder bag, I headed to the bus stop at an unmarked intersection to wait for the van that would take me on the next leg of the journey. The driver was cheery but not too talkative, allowing me space to feel the jitters and excitement for the month of solitude in the dead of winter in the middle of nowhere.

When I arrived at my stop, a town with two stores and one café, a young American nun named Amita was waiting for me outside the café. I recognized her by her shaved head and monastic robes, a yellow T-shirt and maroon skirt. She had a cloth satchel slung over her shoulder and greeted me with a wide smile.

After loading my bags into her Honda Civic, Amita suggested we get some lunch before heading to the abbey, still three hours away. I thanked her for coming so far to pick me up.

"It's my pleasure," Amita said. "I'm thrilled for the break in routine."

"How long have you lived at the abbey?"

"Close to two years. I took temporary ordination a few months after arriving."

"What does that mean?" I asked.

"Most of the monks and nuns that live at the abbey are like me, practitioners who want the experience of monastic life but haven't committed to full ordination. There are only four nuns, like Pema Chodron, who are fully ordained."

"Are there any laypeople like me who stay at the abbey?"

"Not at the moment, but Jerry Chapman and his wife, Susan, are lay practitioners who work at the abbey. He's the head of practice and Susan is the retreat master. You'll meet Jerry soon."

We hastily slurped the last of our lentil soup, then took off for our three-hour ride to the abbey. We chatted amiably between long periods of silence. Amita seemed comfortable with the silence, and I appreciated having space to be with my thoughts and take in the sights. Amita chose Route 19, a more scenic route than the highway, which took us up the west side of Cape Breton Island. We had occasional glimpses of water as we passed through small communities, and as we got closer to Gampo Abbey, I saw moose grazing on the side of the road, as common as deer in my hometown in Marin County. It felt like the end of the earth.

CHAPTER TWO

Arrival

When we pulled up to the abbey, I was taken aback by its starkness. The massive three-story stone building sat alone on a promontory overlooking Pleasant Bay, completely exposed to the elements. Along the driveway, large colorful prayer flags snapped in the wind. Stepping out of the car, I noticed a town way off in the distance and a few cabins tucked into trees down the road.

Amita escorted me to the office of the head of practice, who had interviewed me by phone a few months earlier. Jerry was sitting at his desk when I arrived but leapt up to greet me with a warm handshake. I liked him instantly, his wire-rimmed glasses framing a kind face and balding head.

"Welcome to Gampo Abbey! I hope your journey wasn't too taxing. California is a long way away." He looked familiar to me, though we'd never met, and I felt something deep in my belly relax.

We went over my application, which included my meditation practices—Vipassana, Mahamudra, and the Diamond Approach—and my experiences with silent meditation retreats. He reminded me that stays in the cabins were strictly for deepening spiritual practice, not for writing a book or taking time out from life.

"You have years of experience, and you want to go beyond that here," Jerry said.

"That's my hope," I said, though I wasn't sure what that might look or feel like.

"Let me show you around the abbey before you head to your cabin. The nuns and monks are in the meditation hall, so we can walk around freely without interrupting them."

We meandered through a labyrinth of hallways to get to the kitchen and library, both on the same floor and well-marked. Then we headed downstairs to the basement, where the food storage bins and laundry room were located. To preserve my silence, as well as the privacy of the nuns and monks, Jerry emphasized that I was allowed to visit the abbey only during residents' periods of meditation practice.

"Your boxes arrived last week and are waiting for you in your cabin. It's just across the road. You'll be staying in Pema Chodron's cabin, since she's away."

"Oh, how wonderful! Thank you." Though I appeared calm, inside I was jumping up and down with glee.

"Amita dropped off your luggage. Make yourself at home. I'll stop by your cabin in a week to check in on you, but if you need anything, you know where to find me."

Jerry walked me to the road and pointed me in the direction of my cabin. I could barely contain my excitement as I headed across the road. I had sat with Pema several years earlier at the Berkeley Zen Center, just after she had published her first book. Her simplicity and depth had an impact on me, and

I had hoped to study with her again someday but had never imagined sleeping in her bed, meditating on her cushion, or eating off her dishes.

After I unpacked my groceries in the kitchen of my cabin, I hung a lightweight red Durga shawl over the mirror in the bathroom. Seeing my reflection in the mirror felt like a distraction from my aim of turning inward. And who was going to see me anyway? The shawl was a perfect gift from my sister-in-law, Mame. Durga is the Hindu goddess of strength, protection, and motherly love, a strong feminine presence to grace my retreat. And red is the color of the essential aspect of strength, courage, and vitality in the Diamond Approach, a spiritual path I'd been following for years.

Red was my mother's favorite color. She dressed me in it often as a child and encouraged me to wear it when I was old enough to choose my own clothes. When I refused, just to assert my independence, she would push back. "But you look so good in it!" I didn't wear it again until I was in my mid-forties, when I finally felt free to make choices based on what I wanted, not what she wanted or didn't want for me.

In that spirit, I carried the box of books, photos, and sacred icons into the second bedroom to set up my altar. Across from the sofa bed sat a low, two-tiered bookcase. Each tier was covered with maroon felt and held in place by a piece of glass. A photo of Trungpa hung on the wall above the bookcase. Though he wasn't my teacher, I accepted his presence with a bow, then turned my attention to arranging my altar.

It had been so long since I had packed my boxes that the contents felt like a treasure trove. I spoke into space as I unwrapped each object. "Oh, Rumi's *One-Handed Basket Weaving*. I love that book! My crystal Buddha! Rilke's *Book of Hours*!" I rarely left home without it. I took my time, placing each photo and book on the floor in front of the altar, sometimes pausing to look into the eyes of a teacher's photo. I loved my altar at home, though my meditation table was only big enough to hold a few sacred icons, flowers, a votive candle, and an incense holder. Here I had two whole shelves!

Starting in the middle of the first shelf, I placed a photo of Hameed, the founder of the Diamond Approach, along with a small obsidian stone in front to capture the mystery and depth of his presence. I bowed, a gesture of respect and gratitude, before choosing a book by Jack Kornfield, *After the Ecstasy, the Laundry*, on how to live a spiritual life and still be in the world. He was my first meditation teacher, and I carried his teachings in my heart.

Next, I chose a photo of Dipa Ma, one of Jack's Vipassana teachers who lived in India. She was a living example of a spiritual master who fearlessly practiced mindfulness no matter what was happening in her world. Though I wasn't completely conscious of my choices at the time, I can see now that I gravitated toward spiritual teachers who could teach me what it means to be "in the world but not of it." Deep within my soul I still wondered if I was meant to live a contemplative life in a monastery or bring my spiritual practices into a life in the world like Dipa Ma.

What altar wouldn't be complete without a photo of the Dalai Lama? Even before I studied Buddhism, I admired him for his unwavering dedication to living an awakened, compassionate life. I placed a photo of the Dalai Lama with his arm around Thrangu Rinpoche, with whom I had taken my vows of refuge. Taking refuge in the Buddhist tradition is a commitment to awaken from confusion and to live a life of openness and freedom.

Though I didn't have a photo of Jeanne, my private Diamond Approach teacher, I had a book she gave me as a gift for this retreat: *Novice to Master: An Ongoing Lesson in the Extent of My Own Stupidity*, by Soko Morinaga. It's a hilarious and inspirational book about a young Japanese monk who shares his journey of enlightenment. I had briefly scanned it before adding it to my box for Gampo Abbey and was eager to take my time reading it. I placed it on the lower shelf of the altar, along with a huge tome by my Mahamudra teacher, Dan Brown, *Pointing Out the Great Way*. Stacked on the same shelf were other books of poetry and spiritual teachings and a photo of Dilgo Khyentse Rinpoche, a cherished teacher whom I never met in person but whose book *Primordial Purity* was akin to a bible for me. I imagined sitting each morning in front of my altar and seeing which book called to me to study that day.

One of my students had given me a pop-up book of Tibetan deities, each one accompanied by their mantra. It was colorful and clever, allowing me to display a different Buddha each day if that's what I felt inclined to do. The morning I feared I was getting a cold, midway through the retreat, I opened to the deep blue Medicine Buddha, repeating his mantra until I felt better.

Candles and incense were discouraged inside the cabin, but I had packed a battery-operated candle, which I placed on the top shelf, with my crystal Buddha, a deep red heart-shaped stone, and a few malas, or self-remembering beads. I stepped back, feeling like biblical God at the end of creation, blessing my work and declaring it holy. It was time to rest. I sat on my cushion and dropped into deep meditation.

CHAPTER THREE

Discovery

Later that evening, I bundled up and stepped outside. Like a gauzy white sheet, snow covered the forest that encircled my cabin. I stood on the porch, which was decorated with red and green prayer flags, its light the only illumination. I was trying to get my bearings, having arrived at Gampo Abbey just before the sun went down. The abbey was across the road, but for all that I could tell, it may as well not have existed. If there were lights on, they weren't visible from my cabin, which was tucked in trees a few feet away. I'd longed for this kind of solitude, for time to practice meditation with no distractions. And now I was alone, utterly, which until this moment had been merely a concept.

I turned off the porch light and stood in the darkness, taking a moment to sense the cold of a Canadian night in December, the absence of sounds and people. Nobody to talk to, nobody to take care of, nobody else's schedule to follow for a month. No phone, no internet, no contact with the outside world. I anticipated blissful weeks of freedom from the usual constraints of daily life. I still naively believed that "freedom" meant freedom from the external world, not the inner workings of my mind. I had designed this retreat to expand my realization, to have endless hours to meditate and study spiritual teachings, to drop into my deepest nature without the usual responsibilities of ordinary life. But now, standing on the porch, I had no idea how or if this would happen.

When I was approaching the age of sixty in 2006, I felt a pull toward solitude. That spring, a student gave me a book, *A Cave in the Snow,* the story of a young Englishwoman's quest for enlightenment. In 1976, Tenzin Palmo had secluded herself in a cave in the Himalayas for twelve years, engaged in intense Buddhist meditation.

I imagined myself living and practicing in my own cave in the Himalayas. How long could I survive in such primitive conditions? I was in good physical health, but I'd had back issues for years and I wasn't thirty-three anymore, the age Tenzin Palmo was when she entered her cave. Was there a way to satisfy this deep longing to retreat in a remote area, with complete freedom to practice meditation day and night, without putting myself in peril?

Over the next few weeks, I spent every free moment holed up in my study, looking at retreat centers in the United States and abroad. I stayed up late at night searching the internet for the perfect fit: a detached cabin with indoor plumbing, away from civilization but within a supportive environment. And I wanted snow even if it wasn't a cave in the Himalayas. When I found Gampo Abbey, I knew without a doubt that it was my place. I could picture the abbey, a Buddhist monastery in the Shambhala tradition, sitting on the outermost tip of Cape Breton Island in Nova Scotia. I imagined the calm presence of the principal teacher, Pema Chodron, an elder of the lineage whose teachings I'd followed for years. And I knew snow would be inevitable in December.

Months of planning had brought me to this moment in time. But something more elemental in my soul had been guiding me for years, a flame that sometimes burned brightly, at other times was barely noticeable. As a young girl, I was certain that my destiny was to serve the Divine, though who and what that meant remained a mystery. I veered left, right, lost my way, found my way, lost it again. And always, a smoldering flame that never abandoned me was moving me closer to a life of love and wisdom.

Here at Gampo Abbey was an opportunity to reflect on my life up until this point and to surrender completely to this internal flame, to follow it without knowing where it would take me, to find out once and for all if I was meant to live in the world or spend the rest of my days in a monastery.

CHAPTER FOUR

Soulmates

Early mornings in the cabin were simple: rise and make tea, meditate, prepare a breakfast of cooked apples and oatmeal, clean my dishes, then meditate again. After carefully placing the red teacup on the counter, I'd go to my bedroom to sit at my desk. The window over the desk looked out on birch and pine trees, offering a view of the sea when the morning fog lifted. The desk was clear except for the vermilion leather journal that my friend Mike had given to me as I passed through Boston Logan airport on my way to Halifax.

I say my friend, but Mike was so much more. We met in 1976, when I joined a Transactional Analysis and Gestalt training group in New York City. The experience was life changing, not only because it launched my career as a psychotherapist, but also because it introduced me to the man who would become one of the most important people in my life.

Mike, two years older than me, was tall and handsome with a quick mind, well-read and a magnificent storyteller. He'd plant his sparkly blue Irish eyes on you and make you feel like you were the only person in the room. Everyone loved Mike, who was gay and lived with his partner in Princeton.

I was married and raising my one-year-old son in Stanhope, New Jersey, just an hour north of Princeton.

Our attraction was instant, like opposite poles of two magnets coming together. We met for lunches outside the training group, talking nonstop and marveling at how alike we were. We finished each other's sentences and delighted in our similar views on life and spirituality. Mike and I were both runners and had some of our best talks on five-mile runs through the streets of New Jersey. He was the first person I confided in when I started having problems in my marriage, much as he confided in me as his relationship with his partner began to unravel.

We were not romantic partner material, but "friendship" didn't quite capture the bond between us. We began referring to ourselves as two halves of the same egg, separated at birth. In time, with the help of a psychic, we found a new descriptor: soulmates.

"How long have you known each other?" she asked. It was 1979, a time when our explorations were expanding to include not only psychology but metaphysics.

"Just a few years," I said, "but it seems like we've known each other forever."

"No surprise," said Joya. "The two of you have been together for lifetimes, in various relationships."

I'd heard of past lives, but the concept was still a mystery to me. Did we live these lives sequentially or concurrently? And did we always meet our soulmates in each lifetime? Joya answered my question without me having to ask.

"It's a gift that you've found each other. It doesn't always happen. And just to clarify, soulmates doesn't mean you should be married or live together. It means you have a unique bond, a deep understanding of each other."

"I feel like Rose is my sister, my kin. She gets me, and I get her. I can't imagine life without her in it," said Mike.

"I can't tell you the specifics, but my sense is that you are destined to do something together to save humanity," said Joya.

Save humanity? Sounded lofty and even more mysterious to me. All I knew was that whatever we shared together defied the usual relationship categories. But Joya's certainty that we were soulmates prompted me to do some research. I found one definition that resonated the most, describing soulmates as "a special affinity, understanding, or powerful bond between one person and another. The ineffable experience of being known by and knowing another lends itself to the mythical image of soulmates as two wandering souls finally reuniting."

By the time I sat at my desk with the journal from Mike, we had been friends for thirty-one years. I shared everything with him: dark secrets, heart longings, spiritual insights, petty gossip. We supported each other through dramatic breakups with partners and celebrated the joy of eventually settling into happy marriages.

Before opening the journal, I ran my fingers over the cover, embossed with a Frank Lloyd Wright design. I appreciated Mike's choice, something elegant and geometric rather than pink and flowery with angels or goddesses. He knew me so well. I had already made my first entry on November 30 as I flew from Boston to Halifax, a few brief remarks capturing a mix of anxiety and excitement. Now, on December 2, I was ready to chronicle each day, each realization, each moment of doubt and suffering. This journal was only for myself, and I resolved to be honest and tell the truth, whatever my experience.

What I envisioned was that when I left the grounds of Gampo Abbey, I would be more transparent, with a clearer view to Truth than when I arrived. How I walked in the world and served as a window to True Nature was all that really mattered, for my loved ones, for my students, for my enemies, for all beings, myself included.

CHAPTER FIVE

Entering Silence

The road to Gampo Abbey began long before I embarked on the arduous journey to get to Cape Breton Island. Without the teachings of psychological and spiritual masters that fueled my flame along the way, I would not have been capable of spending a month in solitude doing spiritual practices.

Lying on my bed one afternoon, I contemplated how much I had learned since 1981, when my Reiki therapist at the time suggested I learn how to meditate. A lapsed Catholic searching for meaning, I took that advice and signed up for a weekend Vipassana silent meditation retreat.

I made it to the oceanside at Commonweal Retreat Center, in Bolinas, California, hauling the sleeping bag, meditation cushion, and comfortable clothes I was told to bring. My first task was to climb the hill to a large building where I was told I could deposit my things "wherever you find a spot." Finding that spot wasn't easy amid the sleeping bags scattered all over the floor. I'd mostly dismissed my anxieties as I approached this destination, but I couldn't deny them now. That cement floor looked very uninviting. In fact, it looked dreadful. I considered turning around and heading home.

As I walked back down the hill with my meditation cushion, I could see the ocean off in the distance, a dirt road, and a military building of some sort. But I was headed elsewhere, to the building where participants gathered for instructions about the retreat. Unlike the spare architecture of most of the buildings, this was a stone and wood structure with a covered wraparound porch—a charming, rustic structure where I noticed people visiting in groups of two or three. I knew nobody and stood off to the side, wondering if the time to leave might be before things got started. But then urns of tea and trays of fruit and muffins were placed on a large table under a portico with an invitation to help ourselves. It was four o'clock, so I assumed this was an afternoon snack and that we'd be having dinner later. I didn't want to spoil my appetite and took just a few pieces of fruit and a cup of tea.

After forty-five minutes, someone rang a large bell and announced that it was time to find a spot in the meditation hall for our zafu, or meditation cushion. The meditation teacher, James Baraz, introduced himself and assured us that, during our weekend together, we would receive step-by-step instructions in Vipassana meditation, a concentration practice that uses breath to anchor the mind in pure awareness.

One of the assistants posted a schedule, which included meals, sitting and walking meditation sessions, and times to awaken and times to go to bed. We would enter into silence—no talking allowed. We would keep our gaze downward rather than looking directly at people, to help keep our focus inward. Bells would signal the beginning and end of sessions and mealtimes, and serve as an alarm in the morning.

The first two sessions were challenging. My body was not designed to sit cross-legged on a cushion. I had difficulty finding a comfortable posture and sitting still for the duration of the meditation. When no dinner bell rang and the only respite from sitting was a walking meditation, it dawned on me that what I had thought was a snack was actually dinner. Or what is referred to as Afternoon Tea. After one more sitting session, I went to bed that first night cold and hungry and wondering if I'd made a huge mistake.

Morning breakfast and tea helped change my mood, and I was surprised to find myself looking forward to sitting. The endless silence was soothing, a welcome respite from my usual life filled with conversation. James gave more instructions, and some people asked questions before another walking, then sitting, session. As the morning progressed, I became more comfortable with the instructions but noticed how difficult it was to find silence within. As diligently as I focused on the breath rising and falling, thoughts and images continued to intrude on my concentration. I thought of food and what we might be served at the next meal; I wondered if other participants were as settled as they appeared. I started making up stories about some of them, imagining where they lived, if they were married or single. Each thought took me on a tangent until I realized I was no longer present and had to bring myself back to my breath. But the more I tried to stop thoughts, the more agitated my mind became, and my body soon followed. By Saturday afternoon, I wanted to run from the meditation hall flailing my arms and screaming "Get me out of here!" But the "here" was within, and I soon discovered there was nowhere to run to, no refuge other than continuing to practice.

Sunday morning dawned. I was conflicted about the retreat ending. My body ached but my mind was becoming increasingly settled. And though I enjoyed the silence, I missed conversation. When James mentioned, at the start of the first sitting, that the kitchen needed a few volunteers to cut vegetables but that it would require some talking, my hand shot up. I imagined I'd look forward to talking, but again, to my surprise, I wasn't ready to let go of the silence. I was beginning to see that my mind had lots of ideas that didn't always correspond to my actual experience.

Once we were given instructions, mine to peel carrots, I brought the same concentration to my task as I had been bringing to meditation practice. I peeled slowly, mindfully, taking deep breaths and staying in the moment. The carrots were more orange than I remembered carrots to be. I marveled at the slight patina that coated each peeled carrot, and how beautiful they looked stacked one on top of the other. I was in carrot ecstasy until a bell woke me from my reverie.

Time for walking meditation. I put down my peeler and left the kitchen, out onto the grassy area where other participants were walking. Unlike my first day, I easily dropped into a rhythm—lifting, reaching, lowering, stepping—one foot at a time, one breath at a time, turning after five steps and repeating. When we sat together for the last session before ending silence and conversing with each other over lunch, I noticed a tug toward monastic living that I hadn't felt in years.

When I returned home, I continued to meditate in the mornings before work. I attended a few of James's meditation classes in the East Bay and thought I was well on my way to becoming a Buddhist. But I soon got caught up in familiar routines, and meditation fell away. When my Reiki therapist asked why I had stopped practicing, I rattled off excuses: too busy, too many distractions in my daily life.

"No, really," she asked, "why did you stop?"

I took a few moments before sharing the truth. "I got scared that if I continued, I'd end up in a monastery and have to leave behind everything that I value in my life."

"Well, there's some truth to that," she said. "You will lose something, but it's not what you think. And you don't have to enter a monastery to experience true freedom."

Was it possible to live a spiritual life and still be in the world? The only times I'd felt connected to my spiritual nature involved communion with myself, not others. I couldn't imagine, yet, that sitting with clients, sharing a meal with my family or friends, cleaning the house, or shopping for clothes could in any way be spiritual.

I felt that connection again here at Gampo Abbey. I honestly didn't know if I would return to my home in California as planned in a month, or if I would decide that monastic life was my true path.

CHAPTER SIX

Awakening Compassion

It was the middle of my tumultuous second night at Gampo Abbey, and sleep was nowhere in sight. I stared at the sliver of a black starry sky visible outside my bedroom window. This retreat was not going as planned. I had imagined blissful days and dreamless nights, but my history followed me to Gampo Abbey. As Jon Kabat-Zinn taught in *Wherever You Go, There You Are,* the best thing to do when that happens is to turn toward whatever is right here, right now.

Sage advice, but it wasn't easy to stay in the present moment.

I lay awake in my cabin, sleep eluding me, my mind ruminating on old hurts. I thought about two of my girlfriends in grade school. They lived a few blocks away and sometimes excluded me from playdates. Or they would ignore me in the schoolyard and talk about me behind my back. I felt painfully rejected and humiliated, not knowing what I'd done wrong. I vowed to not let that happen again, though of course it did anyway over the years. But I became sensitive to slights, and if I thought someone I liked didn't like me, I withdrew rather than risk rejection.

As I was immersed in these memories, to my horror, the telescope looking out on those people who hurt me turned and pointed directly at me. I was flooded with a cascade of images of times that I had hurt others with my thoughtlessness, impatience, turning my back on them. With crystal clear awareness, I watched myself roll my eyes in disdain at Al, my first husband, or walk out of a room when I didn't want to talk about something. And there I was getting strident, talking over someone when I thought I was in the right. Just as I had been slighted, I slighted others. Thankfully it never spiraled into physical abuse, but still it was painful to see how I was not simply an innocent victim in my relationships.

I awoke the next morning, still feeling profound sorrow in my heart. I asked whatever benign presence existed in the universe for forgiveness for all the ways I had knowingly or unknowingly hurt people. Whether it was my imagination or reality, I was certain Al met me in a dream realm during the night, his face soft and open as I asked for his forgiveness. *Forgive me, too, for hurting you,* I heard him say. In that moment, we made peace.

It was an unexpected purification process that left me shaken in a good way. Our love and forgiveness of each other felt complete. The burden of the past lightened some, and I savored the momentary taste of true freedom.

Despite my practices of nonattachment—not allowing things to own me—I grew attached to my red teacup. One morning I was so enchanted with it that I drew a picture of it filled with chai and named it "Warm Red Sunrise." As I sipped, I prayed that all beings might enjoy warm coffee or tea drunk from such a lovely cup. I could feel the turmoil of my first week at Gampo

Abbey settling down. The emptiness of solitude was permeating my consciousness. Thoughts became more transparent and my mind more spacious. I was getting glimpses of a life free from the patterning of my history. Sitting in meditation felt as natural as eating and sleeping.

Once a week Jerry, the head of practice, checked in on me. On those mornings I'd brew a large pot of tea, its smell filling the cabin with enticing aromas of cinnamon and cardamom. The cabin was not designed for social visits, so I'd bring an extra chair into my bedroom and use the desk as a table for our teacups. I served Jerry his tea in the large red cup while I drank from one of the kitchen mugs. At first, I felt self-conscious having Jerry in my private space, but soon we were talking as if we'd known each other for months, not days.

"How are you getting along?" he asked at our first meeting.

"Very well." I paused for a moment, gathering the courage to be completely honest. I shared details of my turbulent first week, including the painful memories of being abused by my first husband, as well as the experience of the two of us forgiving each other. Jerry nodded, signaling that he understood.

"Time alone is precious and sometimes yields uninvited insights. How are your practices?"

"I'm more concentrated when I sit, and I chant when I'm walking or cleaning. It helps me land more in the moment."

Jerry suggested that I try the Shambhala practice of tonglen. A method for connecting with suffering—ours, and those around us—the practice starts by taking on the suffering of a person we know to be hurting and whom we wish to help. You breathe in all the pain and fear of that person, and then, as you breathe out, you send out happiness or joy or whatever might relieve their pain and awaken their consciousness.

In theory, tonglen is a simple practice aimed at awakening compassion. In actuality, it challenges the ways we hold ourselves separate from other human beings, the ways we think we are different, better than or worse off than others. I took it to heart and added it to my practice. At Jerry's recommendation, I borrowed Trungpa's pamphlet on the practice when I next visited the library. He described it as alchemy: what you breathe in meets the heart of compassion and transforms negativity through that alchemy.

When I first arrived at the abbey, Jerry had warned me not to wander off the path along the cliff because hunters sometimes illegally shot game in the woods. Most of the homes were unoccupied for the winter, and I had grown accustomed to being alone on the road. One morning I came upon a parked truck, which I assumed belonged to a hunter. I felt a pang of fear but continued walking, hoping my fear would pass. Instead, it intensified. My heart was racing, and I considered turning back. What if a stray bullet hit me? How long would it take for someone to realize that I was missing? What if the truck belonged to a rapist who was hiding in the woods waiting for an unsuspecting woman to walk by? What if he wanted to kill me? I was terrified as I imagined his knife slashing my face before ripping off my clothes, delighting in my suffering.

Suffering.

The word snapped me out of my reverie, like the gong of a meditation bell. I spontaneously began breathing in the pain that would make this imagined man want to rape or torture me.

I breathed in his smoky pain and breathed out white light from my heart, sending him goodness, kindness, whatever might benefit him. “He” became every violent man or woman. “I” became every victim. At first the practice was not entirely pure. I would have flashes of being tortured, and fear would interrupt my breathing. I felt revulsion at the thought of absorbing this violent person’s pain. But I kept returning to the practice, breathing in, breathing out, allowing the alchemy to work its magic. To my surprise, what arose was a sincere willingness to give up my life, if necessary, for the sake of this imagined man’s awakening. The lines between victim and persecutor—myself and my mother, myself and Al, myself and any other—dissolved into deep compassion.

I reflected on what had happened during my first difficult week at Gampo Abbey, when it seemed as if Al and I met in the liminal space between life and death and reached a détente. The visceral sensation of purification arose again in my body, a lightening, a shedding, and it felt as if the air itself was cleansing all living beings of suffering.

This profound realization was reminiscent of one I’d had a little over a year earlier. In 2003 my third, and current, husband, Rich, had attended a meditation workshop at Esalen, the birthplace of humanistic psychology in Big Sur, California. He was so impressed with the teacher that he encouraged me to join him the following year. Dan Brown, a psychologist and Tibetan scholar, had developed a unique way of teaching Mahamudra meditation. Rich was particularly impressed with how Dan taught concentration, something that I was still having difficulty establishing in my practice.

I signed up for Dan's workshop, and when I told Mike about it, he decided to attend too. The three of us spent a week practicing in the meditation hut at Esalen, a dark wooden structure, with a peaked roof, built in the round. The tiny room, surrounded by tall redwoods, sat next to a river leading out to the ocean. What made it special was that it held only twelve participants. In a few years, Dan became a sought-after teacher and outgrew the more intimate venue of the hut. I felt fortunate to be learning a new practice and getting so much individual guidance while meditating with the two most important men in my life.

Dan turned out to be a fierce teacher. He was prematurely gray, with piercing blue eyes and a thick Boston accent. During meditation instructions, his voice was steady and kind. But in between meditations, he did nothing to hide his impatience if a student did not seem to be following the instructions.

"Meditation is not about relaxation. It's a practice of awakening, of bringing clarity and awareness to the mind," he announced on the first night. He gave us an overview of the Elephant Path, a Tibetan practice that teaches the nine stages of concentration, or "mind staying." It starts with working with mental agitation, then finding an object of concentration, and eventually settling into one-pointed concentration. The elephant represents the mind and how dangerous it is if not tamed. Once the elephant or mind is tamed, it rests in calm abiding, which ends the suffering caused by the untamed mind.

As Dan went through the stages that first night, he mentioned one called "subtle laxity," the way the mind gets dull as concentration deepens. I'd never heard the term, but I knew it intimately from my many sittings. I would be concentrated and next thing I knew, I'd space out. What a relief to have someone name where I was getting stuck. I was excited to begin practicing with him the next morning and felt my good fortune to be sitting with yet another master, having already spent time studying with Jack Kornfield and Hameed Ali.

Within days, the turbulent thoughts in my mind settled like particles of sand at the bottom of an ocean. Dan's instructions were at once both unfamiliar and deeply known. Concentration became effortless, everything melting into what is called One Taste: each moment the same taste of emptiness regardless of how it arises. A wormhole opened in my consciousness, reconnecting me to many lives spent in the caves and monasteries of the Himalayas practicing this form of meditation. It was as if I were simply being reminded of practices that lived in my soul. If I had been skeptical about past lives before, I became a believer.

One morning before a meditation session, I decided to take a walk along Highway 1, a narrow winding road in Big Sur that overlooks the ocean. I was walking in the direction of traffic, the only side of the road with a pathway, when I was startled by a loud honking horn from a huge truck coming up from behind. I jumped, not knowing if I had strayed into the road or why the driver was laying on his horn. As he passed by, I had an immediate reaction of anger. *What an idiot, what did he do that for?* The image of the side of his face remained as I stood still, trying to catch my breath. The breathing brought me back into my body, back into presence and with that came the realization that he and I were both scared. He of hitting me; I of being caught unawares while in a vulnerable state. He was no longer the "other," the persecutor, and I was no longer a victim. Compassion for our shared humanity arose spontaneously and stayed with me as I headed back to the meditation hut.

Near the end of the retreat, I experienced what Dan called "crossing over," which happens when the bubble of the egoic self dissolves and what remains is only pure awareness. No stories, no self, complete openness and searing clarity. Only sky, no clouds, so to speak. I had been having experiences of pure awareness over the past two days, but each time I got close to freedom from any sense of self, my mind would reengage, and I'd be back to my familiar identity of Rosanne sitting in meditation, trying to maintain my concentration.

It was the last sitting of the morning before lunch when I had a breakthrough. I could hear Dan giving out instructions, but I was so absorbed in stillness that his words sounded more like musical notes than instructions. That's when I became aware of an almost imperceptible boundary surrounding my consciousness, as though I were sitting inside a transparent bubble. I was aware of people standing up to leave and realized that the meditation session was over. I remained seated, certain that I couldn't have moved a muscle if I'd tried. Dan came up to me and whispered in my ear, "Finish it," then left the meditation hut.

I remained seated, alone, absorbed in the bubble. And then it popped! I sat there in pure awareness, realizing how thin the veil was between egoic identity and freedom. When I opened my eyes, the clarity was searing: colors, shapes as vivid as if someone had applied a fresh coat of paint to the world.

In time, I became aware of my body needing to pee. Slowly I made my way down the dirt path to the bathroom. Before this experience, I hadn't noticed the murals painted on the walls of the bathroom. Now I was mesmerized by their colors and shapes and stood staring at them for what seemed like hours but was probably only ten minutes. I headed to the dining hall, and spotted Dan and his two assistants sitting at a table. When they saw me, their faces broke into wide grins.

"Welcome to reality," Dan said.

I remained mostly silent, but with a big grin on my face too. And in that state of consciousness, I felt love and compassion for them, for the other participants in our retreat including Rich and Mike, for the whole of humanity, myself included.

Though I acutely remember the experience, what affected me more deeply was the realization of compassion while off the cushion, so to speak, like when I was walking on the highway in Big Sur, or while I walked on the road in Gampo Abbey. The immediacy of realization versus a conceptual understanding. It's what brought home without a doubt that human beings are inextricably connected to each other. What happens to one cell in the universe affects all other cells in the universe. If I could forgive those who had hurt me, and myself for hurting others, perhaps that act of forgiveness could touch even a stranger.

Jerry was right. Tonglen was a good practice for me. On the walk back to the cabin I was filled with gratitude for the fortunate and unfortunate circumstances of my life. I thought about the people I had left to come here, my husband, my son, my family, and close friends, my students and colleagues in the Diamond Approach. I felt profound love for all of them, especially my mother. For many years I was certain that she had failed me, that I would have fared better with a mother who believed in me and encouraged me to live my own life instead of thwarting me each time I stepped outside her box. I now realized that she gave me what she had to offer.

Buddhists believe that we choose our parents before incarnation. Did I choose this woman because I needed to learn how to live with the pain of rejection and abuse? My experiences as a child and young adult sensitized me to human suffering, both my mother's and my own. It made me a better therapist, spiritual teacher, wife, and friend. As I matured, I became more compassionate, less hateful. In this regard, you could say my mother was one of my most profound teachers.

As my heart softened toward her, I saw myself as a mother more objectively. I came into this retreat with a certainty that I had failed my son, that he would have fared better with a mother more suited to his temperament, one who had the willingness and skill to set loving limits and not be so distracted by professional ambition. All this was true, but it was an incomplete picture and there was no going back, no rearranging the puzzle of a life. If I took out one piece, or inserted something different, it would be a new puzzle. If I hadn't had the mother I was born to, or the son born to me, it wouldn't be my life. As difficult as my life seemed for many years, given the choice, I would still choose this one.

CHAPTER SEVEN

Impermanence

Gampo Abbey was an exquisite manifestation of impermanence. One moment it was snowing; the next, blue sky peeking out through the clouds, then snow or rain. Grass disappeared under blankets of snow and would magically reappear as temperatures rose. From my desk, the landscape changed before my eyes. A red rock emerged where I'd just recently seen a treed hill. White snow covered its peak, and when the sun came out, it created an illuminated vision of rock and snow.

Once I completed my morning meditations, journaling, and some light housekeeping, it was time to bundle up for a long walk. Other than a Qigong practice, this was my only form of exercise. Temperatures ranged from the mid-thirties to below zero. Some days were calm; on others the wind whipped me around on the single path that hugged the cliff overlooking the water. Some days I turned right, toward the town five miles away.

Most days I turned left, a more scenic walk that crossed a creek dotted with tiny statues of Buddhas and Tara (the Buddhist name of the bodhisattva of compassion) that retreatants had left as offerings. Then up a hill to the giant white Stupa surrounded by colorful prayer flags. Circumambulating the Stupa, I silently chanted "Om Mani Padme Hum," which means "praise to the jewel in the lotus." It's a well-known Tibetan Buddhist mantra that cultivates mindfulness and compassion.

With snow crunching under my boots, I continued down the road for two miles on my way to a clearing where I could stand at the very edge of the cliff. There was a steep path leading down to the water, but I never braved it. Some days the wind was so strong that I feared it would pick me up and dump me into the icy water and no one would know what had happened to me.

By the time I returned to Naropa, the name of my cabin, my fingers and toes would be turning to ice while my torso was damp with perspiration. I had chosen the right coat but could have used heavier mittens and socks inside my boots. Stripping off layers, I'd hang my coat above the heater in the foyer and set my boots close by in preparation for my next outing.

After a light lunch and nap, afternoons were spent meditating, writing in my journal, or reading spiritual books. Then it was time to either do laundry or gather food from the storage bins in the basement of the abbey.

Prior to this retreat, I did not think of myself as an anxious person, but I was almost paralyzed by fear when it came time to go to the abbey. Jerry had told me that I was welcome to help myself to the occasional leftovers in the abbey's main refrigerator. However, when I'd venture into the kitchen, I felt like a thief. It was an enormous room, its walls and ceilings covered with pots and pans and cooking utensils, food preparation zones neatly organized with cutting boards, knives, and storage containers. The mouthwatering scent of spices lingering from the last meal would set my stomach to grumbling. Though I love to cook and am considered quite skilled by my friends and family, I was at a loss as to how to work creatively with the ingredients available in the storage bins: apples, oranges, beans, potatoes, rice, oats, broccoli, cauliflower, carrots, onions, tofu, tuna fish, eggs.

Some days I was obsessed with food, while other days I could not have cared less, as long as whatever I prepared was warm. That said, I still remember going into a state of ecstasy over the miso soup I scored in the abbey refrigerator during my second week, ample amounts of tofu and seaweed swimming in a perfectly seasoned broth. Had I known that it would be the only time I'd find leftovers, I would have taken more, maybe the entire container!

Meanwhile, a critter had boldly taken up residence in the cabin. I'd find turds in empty food containers, in the utensil drawer, and behind the refrigerator, which I had moved during a manic phase of cleaning. One night, when awakened by rustling at the head of my bed, I freaked out and turned on the light to discover the beginnings of a cushy nest of tissues. The critter escaped, but my mind could not stop imagining mice crawling on my head in the dark. *You've crossed a line*, I spoke into the air, removing the tissues and any other soft material from my headboard that might become fodder for a new generation of mice.

Though the silence in my cabin was a great support for staying present, my mind strayed often to the past. I suppose I was trying to make sense of how I'd gotten there.

I could see my young self so clearly now, all of my longings, ambitions, and insecurities. I wish I could have seen myself more clearly back then. I still may have made some of the same choices, but with more self-esteem, I might have felt better about myself even when I made the mistakes I now know are an inevitable part of growth.

PART II
Remembering

She who reconciles the ill-matched threads
of her life, and weaves them gratefully
into a single cloth—
it's she who drives the loudmouths from the hall
and clears it for a different celebration

Where the one guest is you.
In the softness of the evening
it's you she receives.

You are the partner of her loneliness,
The unspeaking center of her monologues.
With each disclosure you encompass more
and she stretches beyond what limits her
to hold you.

—Rainer Maria Rilke,
Book of Hours: Love Poems to God

CHAPTER EIGHT

Seeker

From an early age I was drawn to the sacred. My parents were devout Catholics. We attended Mass every Sunday and more frequently during Lent. As a child, Easter was mostly about chocolate bunnies and colored Easter eggs, but my parents made sure that my two sisters and I understood its religious significance, that Jesus sacrificed his life and then rose from the dead to redeem us. One of the first things we were taught in Catechism class was the concept of Original Sin, the innate tendency of human beings to sin, which we inherited from Adam. It was described as an indelible black mark on our soul and that Jesus's sacrifice made it possible for Catholics to go to heaven when we died, even with that black smudge.

As a way of thanking Jesus for his sacrifice, Catholics were asked to give up something we loved during the forty days of Lent. Candy was an easy choice, since we rarely had it in the house except for holidays. But sweets were a whole other category. Mom baked desserts every night, and I knew if I tried to give them up, I wouldn't last a week. I gave up things like talking back to my mother or teasing my little sister. I never made it through Lent. Dessert might have been the easier choice.

I loved the ritual of Mass, especially on holy days, the altar boys leading a procession to the main altar, swinging censers filled with incense in advance of the priest. As the aroma of frankincense wafted through the church, I swooned with ecstasy. I loved standing, sitting, kneeling throughout the service. I loved holding the leather-bound missal even before I could read. Mom gave me one of her old rosaries that I kept in my coat pocket so that I could work on memorizing the Hail Mary, the prayer repeated as you finger each bead of the rosary.

When I was seven, I received First Holy Communion. This meant I could walk up the aisle with my classmates and kneel in front of the priest as he placed the thin wafer on my tongue. I was careful to let it dissolve rather than chew it or swallow it whole. I kept my eyes downcast as I walked back to my pew, hands clasped in prayer until the last fragment of the host disappeared. The downside of receiving Holy Communion was going to confession, so that our souls would be pure vessels to receive the body of Christ. I was terrified of confession. I wasn't clear on the concept of sin and was afraid I'd leave out one that I should have confessed. To make sure I covered all my bases, I made up a bunch of sins, like lying to my mom or stealing holy cards from my girlfriend, before I walked into the confessional.

Confirmation came next, in sixth grade. It's one of three sacraments of initiation into the Catholic Church along with Baptism and Holy Communion. Although I was only eleven, I knew it was special because the priest made a big deal of telling us that once we were confirmed, we were old enough to receive the blessings of the Holy Spirit. To mark the occasion, each child was asked to pick the name of a saint for our confirmation name.

I chose Teresa of Avila, a famous mystic and poet. She was my favorite saint, and I read and reread about her life in my parents' maroon leather-bound *Lives of the Saints*. Though I didn't consciously understand what it meant to be a mystic, my young soul resonated with Teresa's ecstatic teachings. Her most famous poem has been used as a prayer throughout centuries and is one I return to often over the years.

Let nothing disturb you,
Let nothing frighten you.
All things are passing away; God never changes.
Patience obtains all things.
Whoever has God lacks nothing.
God alone suffices.

My parents, especially my mother, seemed proud of me when I received First Holy Communion and was confirmed. She invited our relatives to the house to celebrate with homemade cakes, coconut cream or a chocolate cake with buttercream frosting, both times. Which is why I was stunned when she slapped me for wanting to become a nun. Not by the slap, but *why* the slap.

Mom was mercurial by nature and had slapped me plenty. One minute she'd be happily sewing clothes for my sisters and me, or costumes for our dance recitals, and the next minute yelling. Maybe I didn't set the table fast enough, or I talked back to her. I didn't see it that way. Any response to her when she was in a mood was considered backtalk. One day she spilled her glass of milk at dinner. In a flash her hand flew across the table and slapped me as she yelled, "See what you made me do!"

My dad, more sanguine than my mother, kept his eyes down and did not interfere when Mom was on a rant. He was reliable, his predictability a sharp contrast to my mom. Every workday, he would come through the front door at 5:20 on the dot. If he promised to pick me and my sisters up from the public swimming pool after work, he would be sitting in the parking lot at 5:15. I adored him, though he didn't say much or spend much time with me.

Even though my mother was unpredictable, I thought she'd be thrilled to find out that Jesus had called me to become a nun. She was a first-generation Italian Catholic who was devoted to the Virgin Mary. She said daily novenas, prayers of thanksgiving or petition to various saints, and her rosary beads were never far from her favorite chair. We didn't have the kind of relationship where I felt safe questioning her, so I never asked her what upset her about me becoming a nun. Maybe she imagined her daughters growing up, meeting good men to marry, her sewing our wedding gowns, and the three of us giving her lots of grandchildren. Becoming a nun did not fit that scenario.

When one of my friends asked me why my mom was mean to me sometimes, the only answer I could come up with was that she was Italian. In fact, I never thought much about how she was or asked her questions about herself. She was my mom, what I was used to, though I did notice that my friends' moms seemed nicer than mine. Elizabeth's mom talked to us like we were adults, sharing stories from the *New York Times* that was always opened, on the kitchen table, to either the crossword puzzle or a story. Gerry's mom let us eat anything we wanted, any time of the day. And baked a turkey every Sunday so that Gerry and her sister could take turkey sandwiches to school for lunch. And Carol's mom let us play alone, without constantly checking on us to see what we were doing.

My sisters didn't fight back with Mom the way I did. Carolyn, two years older than me, stayed under her radar. She offered little resistance to my mother while secretly doing what she wanted to do. When she decided to move to Manhattan with two of her friends after college, she didn't tell my parents until she had moved into an apartment. They learned of her decision in a phone call, too late for them to protest. And when she decided to marry her husband at a civil ceremony in Manhattan, they heard about her decision the same way, in a phone call after the fact.

Janice, six years younger than me, learned how to stay out of the way from watching how volatile Mom was with me. Janice was sweet, quiet, and often left to fend for herself. If my mother raised her voice, Janice would cower in a corner until the storm blew over. She did what she was told to do and didn't talk back the way I did. It took her years to find her voice and express her opinions.

My father was the peacekeeper of the family, doing whatever was necessary to make peace between me and my mother. Mom had the habit of taking to her bed with the door closed after some of our arguments, which often meant a halt to dinner preparations. The scene was always the same, as if on rewind.

"Rosanne, you need to apologize to your mother."

"She started it, Dad, yelling at me for nothing."

"I don't care who started it. Your mother is very upset, and you need to tell her you're sorry."

"But I didn't do anything," I whined. I wanted him to take my side, but he never did.

"Go upstairs right now, Rosanne."

And so I went, seething as I knocked on her bedroom door.

"Can I come in, Mom?"

Low mumbling, the sound of assent.

Lying on her side, under the covers, eyes closed, she ignored me.

"I'm sorry, Mom, for upsetting you."

Standing next to her, I hated her and hated myself for not having the nerve to stand up to my dad.

Eventually she spoke.

"Tell your father I'll be down shortly."

I left feeling humiliated but relieved to not have to talk with her.

Though I remained a devoted Catholic—going to church every Sunday, saying prayers before bedtime—I discovered a new passion near the end of sixth grade: boy-girl parties. The first time I was invited to a party by two of the most popular boys in sixth grade, I was giddy with excitement. As I hung up the phone, I imagined what I would wear: the periwinkle blue dress with the white eyelet ruffle set into the bodice, the only store-bought dress I owned. I'd worn it a few times to church, with black leather t-strap shoes and a garter belt with real stockings.

I hurried downstairs to the basement where Mom was doing laundry, stuffing sopping wet sheets through the wringer of her washing machine with one hand and turning the red crank with the other.

"Guess what!" I shrieked. "Mike and Craig just invited me to their party this Saturday!" I waited for her to join me as I danced around the small laundry room.

She stopped what she was doing. "What did you tell them?"

"I said yes!" Her jaw hardened and her eyes narrowed into slits.

"You didn't ask me first."

"Oh, I'm sorry, Mom. Can I go?"

"No, you didn't ask me first. You'll have to call them back and tell them you can't come."

These were the kids she wanted me to hang out with, the ones from "very good families," and the thought of calling Mike back to say I couldn't come was humiliating. I started to cry. "Please don't make me call them back. Please let me go. I'll never say yes again without asking you first. I *promise*."

She refused to relent. I ran to my room in tears. Then and there, head pressed into my pillow to stifle my wails, my hatred toward my mother solidified in my heart, a hard knot in the center of my chest. *I'll never forgive her for this.* I felt like a helpless, innocent victim of a mean, all-powerful mother, who seemed to take pleasure in bringing me down.

When I was around twelve years old, my mother got furious at me for something I'd said, done, or not done. She started chasing me around the house, with her hand raised to slap me. I turned away from her and headed up the stairs toward my room.

"Don't you dare run away from me. Get back here right this minute young lady!"

My mother was close, on the bottom step, when I turned and raised my hand as if to strike her. Her eyes got wide, and she stopped, her hand mid-air. We stared at each other, then I lowered my hand, turned, walked to my bedroom, and closed the door.

She still yelled plenty after that, but she never hit me again.

My high school boyfriend Tommy was six foot three inches tall, the star of the basketball team and an ace pitcher. He was shy, the child of an unwed mother from the wrong side of the Allentown tracks. Mom did not approve. Tommy and I would neck on the couch in our basement whenever we were left alone for more than five minutes. Which wasn't often. My mother kept tabs on us like a hungry hawk.

One day she walked down into the basement, on the pretense of doing laundry. Luckily, we were just watching television, me with my hand on Tommy's thigh and him with his arm around my shoulder. We had just finished a round of serious petting.

"Rosanne, can you please come into the laundry room? I need to talk to you about something."

She closed the door, and with her face too close to mine said, "Don't you ever touch a boy on his thigh. Do you understand me?"

"We weren't doing anything," I lied.

"I don't care," she said. "Just don't do it."

If she had only known where else my hands had been. Before Tommy, I went to confession once every few weeks. But now each Saturday I snuck off to confession so that I could receive Holy Communion at Sunday Mass. I knew Mom would put the pieces together if I refused communion.

"Bless me Father, I have sinned. I was involved in inappropriate kissing and petting two times this week."

If I saw Tommy on a Saturday night, I wouldn't let him do more than kiss me on the cheek until after I'd gone to Mass. And I never let him go all the way no matter what day of the week. I was still Catholic in my bones and planned on saving myself for marriage.

Despite dating the most popular guy in our class, being a cheerleader, and having plenty of girlfriends, I didn't think of myself as popular or attractive. When I was elected queen of the junior prom, I was sure the vote had been rigged.

CHAPTER NINE

Purpose

Early in my senior year in high school, my father was offered a position in Cleveland, Ohio, to work at a new branch of his company. Dad was a mechanical engineer. Whatever he did, he did with precision and careful reasoning in contrast to my highly emotional mother.

"We're moving to Cleveland this summer. I've already picked out a college for you there, Notre Dame."

Not the big famous Notre Dame in Indiana, but a small liberal arts college in the suburbs of Cleveland. I was livid, having had my heart set on Marymount, a Catholic women's college in Virginia, where some of my friends were planning to go.

"But I don't want to go to that school," I protested.

"It will be better for you. This way you can make friends in Cleveland. And commuting will save money."

"Commuting?" I cried out. Nothing about this plan sounded right for me. I loved my co-ed high school, with over five hundred and fifty students in my class alone. Notre Dame had less than five hundred students in the entire school, all women, and half of them novitiates studying to become nuns.

But I knew that it was hopeless to sway my father once he made up his mind. He had little patience with his daughters questioning his authority. He wasn't harsh, never raised his voice, and only spanked me once. But I felt his disdain whenever I got too emotional or tried to argue with him. The worst thing he ever said to me was "You're just like your mother."

I hated those words! I was nothing like my mother. OK, maybe I looked more like her than either of my sisters, and maybe we both loved music and dancing, and we were both feisty. But like her? She was the bad guy, he was the good guy, and I felt deeply hurt that my dad saw me that way.

I spent the first two years of college commuting, which I hated. I had always imagined college as living in a dorm with a roommate or two and being free to do what I wanted, far from the probing eyes of my parents. Instead, I was living at home just like I always had. My fellow classmates were nice but struck me as provincial. They elected me class president each year, and when I asked one of my friends why, she said it was my accent, that I sounded sophisticated. *Accent?* I had no idea I even had one, though the nasal tone of East Coasters contrasts sharply with the soft vowels of Midwesterners.

My dad dropped me off at school in the morning and picked me up after classes ended. We had words, not really fights, about which radio station to listen to. When the Rolling Stones' "I Can't Get No Satisfaction" came on, he reached for the dial and changed the station, saying,

"That's disgusting."

The sexual innuendo of the lyrics and the style of music were too edgy for him. He preferred the Big Band sound and crooners like Perry Como and Frank Sinatra. I had my own preferences. Hard rock and heavy metal bands like Jethro Tull left me cold, but I loved pop and folk rock and knew all the words to every Joan Baez song.

Near the end of my sophomore year, my parents decided to move back to Allentown. The new company was not working out, and they missed their friends and family. I had a choice: stay at Notre Dame in the dorms or transfer to a college on the East Coast. Though I didn't feel like I belonged there, the promise of not living at home was a godsend. I decided to stay at Notre Dame, where I had made some good friends.

It was during the reign of Pope John XXIII, and two of my favorite nuns often talked about his progressive ideas during class. But when I returned to school for my junior year, those nuns had mysteriously disappeared. Later I found out that the more conservative nuns who ran the Sisters of Notre Dame decided they were a bad influence and reassigned them to grade schools throughout Cleveland. The banished nuns, with the help of the Jesuit priest Daniel Berrigan, eventually joined up with four other nuns and moved to Pueblo, Colorado, to form their own community. With them gone, the school felt more than ever like a convent rather than a college.

In the fall of my junior year, I attended a weeklong retreat led by Father Hugh O'Donnell, a handsome Jesuit priest. The Jesuits, famous for their liberal thinking and charismatic teaching style, offered counseling sessions during the retreat.

Cleveland was still recovering from race riots earlier that year, and Father O'Donnell spoke to us about the need for greater social consciousness in this country. "We could wait for this to happen naturally, or we could legislate change." He advocated for the latter, postulating that if Black and white people were thrown together, people would realize we're all equal in God's eyes.

I sat bolt upright. Something elemental got stirred. I wanted to do something but had no idea what I could do to help. It came back to me later that day—Jesus speaking to me from the cross in fifth grade. I remembered how the classroom was suffused with light and how happy I was when it happened. *Maybe that's it. Maybe I should enter the convent.* My fellow classmates who were postulants seemed happy enough, and I longed for something more meaningful in my life.

I scheduled a private interview with Father O'Donnell for the next day.

We met in the smoker, a casual living room in the basement of my dorm. In those days, girls weren't allowed to wear pants on campus. I wanted to dress respectfully for the interview, so I showed up wearing a black straight skirt, tall black boots, a tan turtleneck, and my favorite herringbone blazer. Out of habit, I brought my cigarettes, but as I entered the room, I regretted it, thinking it sacrilegious to light up in front of a priest.

I introduced myself, and, as we settled into the lumpy couch, Father eyed my cigarettes. When he told me to feel free to smoke, I declined. I couldn't imagine going through the motions of inhaling and blowing out smoke anywhere near him.

After a few exchanges about his talk the day before, I told Father that I was thinking again about entering the convent, something I hadn't thought about since I had a vision in fifth grade.

Father O'Donnell leaned forward and looked at me intently.

"What kind of a vision?"

"I thought Jesus moved on the cross and called me to serve him by becoming a nun."

"Did you tell anyone about it? Your teacher? The parish priest?"

"No. Only my mom. She slapped me across the face and told me to never mention it again. You're the first person I've told since then."

"Did you have any more visions?"

"No, but I feel restless, as if I've lost my way."

Father asked how I spent my free time, and I told him about hanging out with my girlfriends, going to dances at John Carroll, and playing bridge in the smoker.

Father sat quietly for a few moments. When he spoke again, he was kind but firm. He told me that he didn't know why my mother had reacted the way she did but that I didn't need to become a nun to make a difference in the world.

"It's an equally high calling in God's eyes to become a wife and mother. I'm sure, if you search, you'll find other ways to serve the Lord that are more suitable to your temperament."

My temperament?

Then he stood up, signaling the end of our interview. I stood, too, and shook his outstretched hand.

"Can I offer you one piece of advice?" he asked. "When you apply eyeliner, consider extending it beyond the end of your eyelid. Your face can carry it."

He gave me a tiny smile and walked out of the room.

Father O'Donnell's response left me as baffled as my mom's. If my true desire was to serve God, I was coming up against a Do Not Enter at the door of convent life. Twice when

I reached out for guidance, I got little by way of understanding whatever this pull was that made me think I wanted to become a nun.

Years later in therapy, I pondered what my mother's reaction was about. I was her "chosen one," the daughter who would fulfill her unfulfilled dreams, and becoming a nun was not one of them. But Father O'Donnell remains a mystery. Was he being seductive? Was he gay? Or was he a man who'd missed his calling as a makeup artist?

What I believe now is that I heard my own inner voice of guidance in fifth grade. Being a good Catholic girl and the child of a barely middle-class family, I had a limited repertoire of how to envision a call to service. The most I could imagine was becoming a nun, a nurse, or a teacher until I married and had children. I needed to get away from my family and the church to discover a life that truly reflected who I was and how to serve humanity. The world was changing rapidly in 1967, and soon most everything that my parents and I valued would get thrown out in pursuit of freedom. It was in that maelstrom that I floundered as I tried to find my way.

CHAPTER TEN
Freedom

After graduating from Notre Dame College, I accepted a job as a caseworker at Allentown General Hospital. My parents' next-door neighbor was the administrator and had graciously offered me a summer job after my junior year of college, in the casework department. It was my first "real" job, not like babysitting or selling hot dogs at the concession stand at the public swimming pool, and I got high marks for my work.

The downside was that I would be returning to Allentown. When I told my parents that I wanted to live in my own apartment, Mom's response was, "What are you planning on doing in your own apartment that you can't do here?" She didn't expect an answer. I decided not to argue, knowing she would scoff if I said, "My freedom."

Eight months into the job, the psychiatric social worker quit in a huff, and I was asked to fill his position until the hospital could hire a social worker with a master's degree. It was an easy job, doing intakes in a spacious Victorian office, a far cry from my basement cubicle in the social work department. I did the math. With a master's degree, I could earn twice as much, with the bonus of a get-out-of-Allentown-free ticket. The experimental sixteen-month program at Rutgers was appealing, plus they offered me a full scholarship and stipend from the VA Association, on the condition that I complete my fieldwork at the VA hospital in Lyons, New Jersey.

Dad insisted on driving with me to look at an apartment and interview the woman who would become my roommate. I often wonder why I complied. Out of habit? I was twenty-one years old, a college graduate with a responsible job at the Allentown Hospital Social Services Department. I suspect it was because I still felt like a dutiful little girl around him.

Dorothea was a few years older than me, drove a vintage BMW, and was fastidious and humorless. My bedroom was right off the kitchen, so not very private, with a tiny window, a dresser, and a single bed. The apartment and Dorothea struck me as dark and dated, but my father approved, shaking Dorothea's hand with a friendly, "Keep an eye on her." I wasn't so keen on the setup, but anything was better than living with my parents.

In September 1969, two years after the Summer of Love, I unpacked my bags, set up my GE Swingmate record player on top of the dresser, jumped into my tan VW bug, and headed to the Rutgers campus for my first day of classes. Even though I smoked a pack of Marlboros a day and had recently lost my virginity to a boy I had known since grade school, I was "a good girl" relative to what was happening in American culture. I was a people pleaser, avoiding conflict whenever possible except with my mother. I showed up for work on time and did more than was asked of me. I never skipped classes or homework in high school and college. I respected the rules of society and rarely drank alcohol. Now women burned bras, marijuana and LSD replaced alcohol as the high of choice, and marriage was no longer considered a prerequisite for lovers to live together. It wouldn't take me long to catch up.

Away from my mother's prying eyes, I was determined to find myself, to live my own life. But my view of autonomy was naive, believing that it meant being free to do whatever I wanted to do without having to answer to a higher authority. Without much practice in decision-making, I was more reactive than proactively free. "Not my mother" was my guiding principle.

I grew my thick wavy dark brown hair down to my shoulders and secured its wild curls with a leather headband, Hippie style. Even though I thought my thighs were fat, I wore miniskirts and knee-high boots and low-slung bell-bottom jeans, which accented my tiny waist. I marched on Washington, got a prescription for birth control pills at the insistence of a friend, and had worry-free sex with a few guys. I smoked pot, listened to Leonard Cohen, the Band, and the Beatles. I still thrill at the memory of long strands of hair whipping across my face as three of us girls piled into the front seat of my friend's Racing Blue MGB, top down, blasting "Abbey Road" and speeding through the streets of town. With the Catholic Church in my rearview mirror, thoughts of becoming a nun or pursuing anything spiritual disappeared.

Alphonzo, seven years older than me, was charismatic, bright, handsome, and Black. When we met, he was living in married housing at Rutgers with his second wife and young child. Included in his mystique was the fact that he had played professional football for the New York Jets with Joe Namath. Born and raised in a poor section of Washington, DC, Al, as everyone called him, had high aspirations to escape the fate of his six siblings, who could never afford to move out of their neighborhood. He pursued me vigorously at a dance party, cutting in on the guy I was dancing with and pulling me close as he declared that we were destined to be together.

"What about that wedding ring?" I asked.

"We've decided to separate, just working out some details." I was put off by his arrogance but didn't pull away. He had a boldness about him that intrigued me, and a stutter that offset his cockiness. Over the next few weeks, he confidently joined me when I was walking to classes or eating in the dining room.

Besides his positive, fun-loving qualities that made him very likeable, my attraction to Al might have had something to do with wanting to be like my older sister, Carolyn, who had married a Dominican. Her marriage looked adventurous to me, worlds apart from my staid white upbringing. I admired her ability to circumvent my parents' control and thought she was courageous. It wasn't until years later that she told me what drove her behavior.

"It never occurred to me to share anything about myself with anyone."

She lived in her own bubble, perhaps her way of coping with our overbearing parents.

Six months after Al and I began dating, he moved out of married housing, and the two of us rented an apartment together. Despite the cultural revolution we were in the midst of, we decided to go the old-fashioned route and get married after graduation. I was still Catholic in my heart.

Mom was sitting at her sewing machine in the basement of our family home, hemming a pair of pants, when I told her about Al. I wanted to share my news in person rather than over the phone.

"Mom, I've met the man I'm going to marry."

She stopped pushing the pedal of her sewing machine, the absence of whirring deafening. She looked excited as she turned to face me.

"He's getting his master's in social work, too, at Rutgers. And he used to play football with Joe Namath. Wide receiver." I could tell by her smile that she liked hearing he might be famous, even though he had played pro ball for only two years.

I was working up to the difficult part. "And he's Black."

In a flash, Mom picked up her large sewing shears, cocked her arm, and aimed them straight at me. The two of us froze while she considered the option of following through on her swing. Then she slammed the scissors down on the sewing machine and turned her back to me, refusing to look at me as I babbled on about how she would really like him once she got to know him. Eventually I stopped talking and left her at her sewing machine. She didn't speak to me again for the rest of the weekend.

Over the next several months, my parents tried to talk me out of the marriage. Dad took the lead, writing an impassioned five-page letter asking me to consider how "dating a colored boy and even thinking of marriage is not considered in good taste in this society."

A year into graduate school and my burgeoning sense of autonomy, I was enjoying making my own decisions even if some of them were more rebellious than autonomous. And being concerned about what was in good taste struck me as antiquated.

When I refused to call off the wedding, Dad arranged an intervention of sorts with my favorite aunt, Emma, his sister and my godmother, and her husband, Walter. We met in our living room, the four of them taking turns pleading with me to reconsider or attacking me for my lifestyle choices. When my uncle called me a slut for living with Al, not knowing that his daughter was also living with her boyfriend, I walked out of the room and left Allentown more determined than ever to follow through with this marriage.

Up until that moment, I had acquiesced to my father's demands: his choice of where I went to college, which apartment to rent when I left for graduate school. But I had acquired a taste for freedom and wasn't ready to go backward. For better or worse, I wanted to make my own choices.

After three years of marriage, I was ecstatic to learn I was pregnant. At the same time, though, I was beginning to see that as charismatic as Al was, he had a dark side like my mother. He could turn on a dime if he felt slighted and become verbally abusive. A serious crack in the crucible of my marriage occurred during the fourth month of my pregnancy. Al and a friend had been discussing forming a business together, and the friend decided, in the end, to exclude Al. When he found out, Al was enraged, believing that he had been used for his knowledge and then discarded. We were still living in our apartment in New Brunswick but had recently closed on a condo a few towns north. I was blissfully packing sweaters, having just felt the first flutter of movement earlier that day.

Al paced the floor, weaving in and out around the boxes, unable to stand still.

"I have an uncle in prison who could arrange to put a contract on Ben."

This was the first I'd heard of his uncle and, up until that moment, the closest I had ever been to knowing anyone in prison. It was so outside my frame of reference that I thought Al was joking. I stopped packing.

"Seriously? You're kidding, right?"

He glared at me. "I'm dead serious. Nobody pulls a fast one on me. He's going to pay for this."

In a panic, I began pleading with Al to be reasonable, the way I used to plead with my mother when she got irrational. He swung his arms in the air, brushing off my pleas as if they were irritating flies, and continued spitting out disparaging epithets aimed at his friend. Desperate, I changed tactics.

"If you do anything to hurt Ben, I will never speak to you again."

Al walked out of the bedroom and slammed the door. Even though I was alone now, I still felt terrified and hid inside the double closet with sliding mirrored doors. Standing in the dark, holding my growing belly, I tried to catch my breath. *What am I going to do? What kind of a maniac did I marry?* Though I was acutely aware of our racial differences, which added mystique to the relationship, I hadn't taken into account our cultural and psychological differences. Me, a psychotherapist who mined history for a living, had discounted our different backgrounds. Al, raised by a single working mother in a DC ghetto, had often been left alone to fend for himself. I, on the other hand, had been raised by overprotective Catholic parents, in a middle-class neighborhood, and was rarely without adult supervision. Given where we each came from, it was no wonder that we viewed the world differently.

The next crack came on a Saturday afternoon when Greg was six months old. I came home ten minutes late from the Family Counseling Agency where I was working part-time. Al was in his tennis whites and met me at our front door, tossed Greg at me, and warned me that I better not ever be late again. He slammed the door and headed across the street to the tennis courts in our development. I dissolved into tears, feeling powerless, like I did as a child when my mother raged at me. I strapped Greg into his baby chair on the kitchen counter and began washing dishes. While talking baby talk to my son, my mind was racing. I was in a panic and felt trapped. *What to do?*

I continued washing dishes, absorbed in the task.

And then I had a moment of clarity.

Wait a minute, I'm an adult. He's not my father, he's not my mother, he doesn't get to tell me what I can and can't do.

When I realized that I could support myself and my child alone, I stopped what I was doing while my mind did the calculations: how many hours I'd need to work each week to afford rent, food, and a babysitter. In that moment of grace, my consciousness dropped underneath the noise. It was the voice of guidance, connecting me to my inner depth. The same voice I heard in fifth grade.

When Al walked in the door, he encountered a different woman.

"If you don't go into therapy for your anger issues, I'm leaving you and taking Greg with me."

"I'm sorry," he said. "But I have no idea how to find a therapist." Al's degree was in community organization, and he had little knowledge of the world of psychotherapy. It was the '70s.

Boundaries, even in therapeutic circles, were loosely held. I referred him to Mike, not the wisest choice, but it sparked Al's interest in Transactional Analysis. He decided to join his own training program, traveling to Watsonville, California, three times a year. Eventually Al ended therapy with Mike and became a Transactional Analyst himself. When he started attending yearly Transactional Analysis conferences with me, we'd hang out with Mike and my friends from my training group in Manhattan.

Many of our mutual friends attended the Montreal Transactional Analysis conference in 1978, but for some reason Mike decided to skip this one. Before flying to Montreal, Al and I dropped Greg off with the Newsteads, his "second family." One of the teenage daughters or their parents had been watching Greg since I'd returned to work at the Family Counseling Agency.

After three days of meetings and workshops, it was time to party. Al and I took a few hits of pot, de rigueur for the times, and headed down to the banquet hall. Large round tables seating ten were positioned on the periphery of the dance floor. We spotted Betts, a close friend from my training group, already at the table with her husband, Jerry. I ended up next to a guy named Bill from Wisconsin, and we got into a lively conversation about a developmental theory he was working on. Al seemed to be having a great time, taking photos of all of us at the table.

As the dessert dishes were being cleared, Al asked me to come to the room with him to put his camera away before the dancing began. Once we were in the room, his jovial mood shifted.

"What's going on between you and Bill?"

"What do you mean 'What's going on with Bill and me?' We were just talking about a book he's writing."

"Don't lie to me. Are you two having an affair?"

"Are you crazy?"

In a second, he flew across the room and began pummeling me with his fists. Covering my head with my arms, I cried for help, but it was futile. We were staying in a luxurious old hotel with thick walls, and everyone on our floor was downstairs at the dance.

When he stopped hitting, I collapsed. The pain in my arms and across my shoulders was excruciating. I think I went into shock. *Did my husband just beat me up?* Al was instantly remorseful, and I could see that he was scared. He helped me into the bed and warned me not to call anyone while he fetched ice for my arms, which were already turning purple. When the door clicked shut, I kept looking at the phone. I desperately wanted to call Mike, but what could he do in New Jersey? Should I call the front desk and ask them to page Betts? I was too scared to do anything. When Al returned to the room, administering ice and aspirin, I kept my eyes closed. I couldn't bear to look at his face.

Early the next morning, my arms and upper back swollen and bruised, we packed our bags in silence and left the hotel without a word of goodbye to our friends. The only thing I remember saying to my husband on the plane ride home was, "You know this means I have to leave you." He was contrite, as he had been each time he'd lost his temper with me. I assumed he agreed that we were over, but I was not interested in engaging in further conversation, so I don't know what he was thinking or feeling.

Two days after we returned from Montreal, I phoned Mike and told him what had happened.

"He did what?" But before I could answer, he continued. "I was afraid of something like this. He's a maniac."

"He's being really nice right now, but I don't trust him anymore."

"Pack a bag. I'm picking you up in two hours and we're going to Betts and Jerry's for the weekend."

I hesitated, and then said OK. I knew I had to get out of there and that I could trust Greg with his dad. Despite his abusive behavior with me, Al was a devoted father to his daughters from his first marriage, and to our son. His innate curiosity and sense of adventure made him a favorite with children, and Greg adored his playful nature. I, on the other hand, took life very seriously, and could get stern and rigid, like my parents, making it hard to lighten up sometimes when Greg misbehaved.

Three hours after Mike picked me up, we were sitting around the outdoor pool with Betts and Jerry, drinking wine and getting stoned. I cried as I relived the horror of Montreal, and together, we mapped out a plan for my separation and divorce. I was making enough money to support Greg and me in my private psychotherapy practice that I had opened in 1977. I exhaled for the first time in days. *There's a way out. I'm not trapped.*

On a whim, Betts and Mike took me shopping at Bloomingdale's nearby and bought me a pair of red suede strappy Charles Jourdan stilettos with rhinestone insets along the back of the heels. They screamed with the promise of better times ahead. I left the shoes with Betts, promising to fetch them after my divorce.

Emboldened, I went home and announced to my husband that if he didn't move out in two weeks, I would leave with Greg. I was standing on the stairs leading to our second floor, and Al was on the landing looking up at me. It was eerily reminiscent of the time I raised my hand when I was twelve years old to strike my mother, which ended her physical abuse.

"I'm not going anywhere. We can work this out. It won't happen again unless you provoke me."

His menacing tone made my stomach contract in fear, but I wasn't about to cave in. The only decision on the table was who stayed in the house and who left.

I wonder now where I found the courage to stand up to him, but I knew I couldn't live with someone who was intent on slapping me down. I'd had enough of that growing up with my mother. When Al didn't budge, I found a seven-month furnished winter rental on a small lake up the road, packed clothes for my son and me, and moved out a week later.

CHAPTER ELEVEN

Separation

When Al and I separated in 1978 and I moved into the house on Cranberry Lake, I was stretched to the limit of my resources. I had become a certified Transactional Analyst and opened a private practice near my home in Stanhope, New Jersey. The practice filled up quickly, and soon I was juggling motherhood, seeing clients, and attending psychotherapy workshops.

Early in my marriage with Al, at the age of twenty-six, I took the first step on my professional path when I was hired as a social worker in a Family Counseling Agency. My very first client, a forty-two-year-old alcoholic and heavy smoker, leaned across my desk and blew smoke in my face. Then, in a raspy voice, she asked, "And just what in *hell* do you think you're going to teach me about anything?" Though she struck the fear of God in me, I felt a quickening. I took a drag on my own cigarette and, as I exhaled, said, "Let's find out, shall we?"

I'd found my footing for the first time since Mom slapped me in fifth grade for wanting to become a nun. *This is what I'm meant to do,* I thought. I felt at home the minute I sat behind that oversized mahogany desk and couldn't believe I was getting paid to do what I loved, which was listening to people's stories and helping them make sense of their lives.

Marrying a divorced man was considered a mortal sin, and once I had signed that marriage certificate, I was unceremoniously excommunicated from the Catholic Church. Psychology and human consciousness became my new religion. Over the course of my young professional life, I pursued the latest innovations in psychotherapy. Freud seemed staid compared to Eric Berne, Fritz Pearls, Carl Rogers, and Alexander Lowen, all leaders in the Humanistic Psychology Movement. I wanted to learn from all of them.

But it was Transactional Analysis that most captivated me. After attending an introductory weekend in Manhattan during my last semester of grad school, I was mesmerized by this revolutionary method. Eric Berne, a trained Freudian analyst with a rebellious spirit, soon tired of psychoanalysis, with its lengthy process of sitting on a couch for years and very little interaction with the therapist. Transactional Analysis and his book, *Games People Play,* were just catching on among traditional therapists. The workshop took place in the instructor's living room, in a large apartment on the Upper West Side. She drew three large circles, one on top of the other, on a flip chart, then filled them in with PARENT, ADULT, CHILD. She explained that they represented our three ego states and that our human interactions and communications came from any one of these states. It made immediate sense to me, how I ended up in arguments or misunderstandings and how I might be able to help my clients understand their own interactions. *Brilliant,* I thought, and determined to join a training group once I was more settled in my career path.

I was beginning to see where my career would take me, but I was lost in the drama of my home life. The Cranberry Lake house served as a respite where Greg and I stayed for the winter while I got my bearings. I rescued two black kittens that someone had thrown into the lake, and they rescued me. My heart cracked open when I saw them curled up with my three-year-old son in his beanbag chair, wearing his favorite Spider-Man pajamas.

Most days I went through the motions of living but was still in shock. I stared at the lake for hours as the sun rose, drinking coffee while Greg watched *Sesame Street* and *Mr. Rogers*. The snow geese swam on the lake until it froze over. I bought a pair of skates for Greg and found a shovel under the deck to clear the ice of snow. It was one of the few pleasures of that time, teaching Greg to skate and feeling the thrill of gliding across the ice as I had as a child.

The Newsteads, who had watched Greg when I first returned to work part-time, came through again. One of the daughters, Michelle, stayed with Greg when I took on more evening private clients. Al and I shared custody while our attorneys worked out a divorce agreement. He refused to pay any child support during the negotiations, which dragged on for a year. In the end, I received barely enough to cover my rent.

It was a contentious divorce, and I wish I could say I shielded Greg from my hatred, but I did not. I argued with Al in front of Greg and talked about him derisively to my sisters and friends. Chagrined, I watched myself move around Steve Karpman's Drama Triangle, a dynamic model from Transactional Analysis of social interaction and conflict that identifies three roles: rescuer (let me help you), victim (poor me), and persecutor (it's all your fault). Shifting from one role to another is what keeps the drama going. The only way off the triangle, or the wheel of samsara as Buddhists would say, is to disidentify with any role. I could not see myself clearly enough to get free of my own part in the drama.

Historically I identified as either the rescuer or the victim and put the blame for my misery squarely on my mother's and my husband's shoulders. What's true is that they were abusive. And what's also true is that, although I vociferously complained to others about them, I had difficulty standing up for myself and setting boundaries in their presence. On the few occasions that I did, it was empowering, but I avoided most shows of assertion. I equated assertion with aggression and did not want to be like my mother.

Several months after my separation from Al, Mike decided to leave his partner and rented a house in Princeton, allowing us to spend more time together. When the rental on Cranberry Lake was up, I moved into a house in Peapack, New Jersey. Mike promised to help me take care of Greg. But within four months, he was offered an opportunity to join our friend Ginny's psychotherapy practice in Boston.

Ginny, along with Betts and Mike, were close friends from our Transactional Analysis training group. The four of us called ourselves "The Stroke Buddies," a riff on Eric Berne's concept of positive and negative attention, which he called strokes. At training sessions, we hung out together while covertly competing for Mike's attention. We joked about who we were in relation to Mike: Ginny the wife, Betts the sister, me the lover. Each of us wanted to believe we were number one in his heart.

When Mike accepted the offer from Ginny, I was hurt and felt abandoned, believing that Ginny had won the competition. Mike got furious, insisting it was strictly a business move and that he'd always wanted to live in either New York City or Boston. It was our first argument. Both of us being risk averse, we didn't get to the bottom of the real issue that would eventually result in a rupture in our relationship. Instead, we swept the discord under the carpet and stayed in close touch with weekly phone calls and occasional visits. Within a year, I moved to the other side of the country. It would be years before I realized that in part, the move was an attempt to hurt him the way he had hurt me.

On September 19, 1979, I married for the second time at the Swedenborgian Church in San Francisco. You might say I was a runaway bride, running from the shame of my divorce and the pain of Mike's move to Boston, right into the arms of a man named Bob. The basis of the relationship was as unexamined as, "You're from San Francisco? I think I love you."

We met at a conference for Transactional Analysts in Snowmass, Colorado, a year after my divorce. Mike was there too. We'd both been accepted into an advanced training program and were heady, not just from the altitude but from hobnobbing with some of the legends who had developed Transactional Analysis with Eric Berne. I fell in love with the Rockies, the wide-open vistas, bright blue skies, and vowed to move West.

Within eight months of meeting and a few cross-country passion-fueled visits, Bob and I loaded a U-Haul for the long drive cross-country from New Jersey to California to prepare for our wedding. Greg stayed behind with his dad, giving Bob and me time to settle into our new apartment.

We stopped overnight in Omaha, Nebraska, to stay with Mike's family. He'd shared lots of stories about his big Irish Catholic family, especially his mother, and I was looking forward to meeting the Ward clan. Mike was visiting for the week, so it was an opportunity for us to see each other.

Mike was not fond of Bob. He found him obsequious and not entirely genuine. He also thought Bob was too old and set in his ways for me. There was some truth to that, but I was grateful for Bob, who seemed a gentle soul, in contrast to Al's aggressiveness, and he was kind enough to embrace my son as well as me. Bob had written a book of poems and offered to read a few of them to Mike's mom and two sisters, who were swarming around Bob like bees to honey. As Bob read, Mike pulled me aside and whispered how he felt like puking when he watched "the girls," as he called them, fawn over Bob, and made gagging signs behind Bob's back. I stifled a laugh, acutely aware of how much I preferred Mike's company to Bob's. I wished it was us running away to start a new life, not me and Bob.

Neither of my sisters attended the wedding, but my parents and Mike did, though in most of the photos he looked like he was at a wake. The one exception was a candid shot of the two of us, Mike gazing lovingly into my eyes, his hand resting on my upper arm while I returned his gaze, my arm reaching out to touch him. If, as a stranger, you happened to wander into the garden of this wedding, you would swear that he was the groom and I, his bride. Photos don't lie even when we hide the truth from ourselves.

The marriage lasted three years, long enough to leave me feeling humiliated once again and reluctant to embark on another relationship, let alone a marriage. I didn't realize at the time that even though a second failed marriage would trigger a dark night of the soul, it would also catapult me into the beginning of my spiritual awakening. For this, and for bringing me to San Francisco, I remain grateful to Bob.

CHAPTER TWELVE

Running Away

After my first silent retreat in 1981, I was running, literally and emotionally, from what felt like the wreckage of my personal life and the ineffable pull toward a spiritual life. I was now a twice-divorced single mother, managing a full-time private psychotherapy practice and profoundly depressed. I'd wake each morning wanting to go back to sleep, not wanting to face another flat day. I felt exhausted the moment my foot hit the floor, going through my routine, present only enough to appear as if I cared.

Five mornings a week, I'd run three to five miles in Golden Gate Park, then wake my son, feed him breakfast, and walk him the few blocks to his school, and then get myself ready for my first client. I had converted the parlor of our flat into a home office, which allowed me to see seven clients a day, with a break for lunch. I hired a teenage boy to help Greg with his homework until my last client left and it was time to prepare dinner.

I had been a therapist for fifteen years but avoided private therapy sessions, except for a few months when I was having difficulty in my first marriage. I engaged in plenty of group therapy sessions as part of my training to become a Transactional Analyst. My training group met in our trainer's living room in

Manhattan, using each other as guinea pigs to learn how to do regressive therapy. We beat pillows, hit each other or the floor with foam bats called batakas. I screamed, I sobbed . . . I was a big crier then and still am. I sat in stunned silence when the trainer told me that my father was not the idealized dad I had imagined, because he let my mother abuse me. I don't think I said another word for the rest of that session, not wanting to face what I knew to be true.

After I had been practicing for a few years, I joined a training program in Bioenergetics. I had a few private sessions with the trainer, and I dozed off during each one. He droned on and I think he, too, dozed off, but through him I learned of a Reichian therapist, Peter, in San Francisco. Bioenergetics and Reichian therapies were designed to work directly with body armor, and ideally, clients did sessions in their underwear. I had never thought myself a prude but drew the line at taking off my clothes in training or private sessions.

The first few years of therapy I mostly complained about and raged against my mother. I hated her but couldn't seem to separate from her. I beat myself up mercilessly for my own failings as a mother, not being able to distinguish her judgments about me from mine about myself.

Most sessions began with me giving Peter a recap of events since we last met. Sometimes we just talked, but more often than not, at a certain point Peter would say, "Time for mat work." It was my signal to move to an area behind a room divider that had a double-sized bed. Though it was what I had signed up for, I felt resistance each time I lay down on the mattress, knees up, and began taking deep breaths into my belly and chest before exhaling completely. Peter would give various directions, depending on what he was observing, or what I was experiencing as my breathing deepened. Over the years I flailed, had temper tantrums, shouted "Fuck you" and "I hate you." And I made myself vulnerable, holding out my arms reaching into thin air for the love I thought beyond my reach. But through it all, I kept my clothes on.

The day Peter broached the subject again, he asked if I was curious about my resistance to working in my underwear.

"Not really," I said. "What difference does it make if I'm fully clothed or not?"

We were sitting in chairs, facing each other.

"What I can't see is how your skin tone changes when you take deep breaths or do bodywork. It's another layer of information for me. And of vulnerability for you."

Why *was* I resisting? I didn't know but decided to give it a try. I headed to the mattress behind our chairs, took off my clothes, and lay on my back with my knees up, assuming the usual posture for bodywork. I felt self-conscious, but less so than I had anticipated. After all, I'd trusted Peter with so many of my secrets, why not my body in underwear?

Peter gave the usual instructions, asking me to take deep breaths in through my nose, then exhaling out through my mouth. As my breath rate increased and my state began to alter, I panicked, feeling a loss of control. I'm not sure why I thought being fully clothed protected me from whatever might come to the surface, but I did.

"I'm scared," I said.

"You're doing fine. You've breathed like this hundreds of times and nothing bad has ever happened. I'm sitting here in my chair, just like always. Keep breathing," he said.

I had no idea what I was afraid of, but the only way to find out was to stay with it. Eventually the fear gave way to deep, uncontrollable sobs that seemed to come from the very core of my being. The sorrow was ancient and endless, and I felt totally helpless and alone. When the tears subsided, I let my legs slide down as Peter covered me with a blanket. I lay quietly on my back, taking time to notice my various physical and emotional sensations. My usual body tensions had dissipated. I felt soft and open and vulnerable. And curious about the depth of sorrow I had experienced while doing the breathwork.

After I dressed and was sitting back in my chair across from Peter, we talked about what feelings might be underneath my depression. I knew the story of my birth, that my mother had almost died from hemorrhaging and then, two weeks later, had to be rushed back to the hospital when she hemorrhaged again. I knew that she stopped nursing when this happened and that my Nonna took over care of me and my two-year-old sister while my dad worked and visited Mom in the hospital. I knew that I refused the bottle and that I had difficulty keeping down any formula. And that Nonna, fearing that I would die of starvation, poured formula down my throat from a shot glass. Could this be the source of the sorrow I had just tapped into?

At the time, it didn't seem possible, and it would be years later, when I went back into therapy, that I learned about abandonment depression. But in that moment, with Peter, at that time in my life, I wasn't ready to explore it more deeply. I wanted to get over it, get on with my life and stop feeling so miserable. I hadn't yet embraced the wisdom of no escape: that there is no "getting over," only going through adversity to heal old wounds.

Meanwhile, during my runs in Golden Gate Park, I'd pass a group of Asians practicing Tai Chi or Qigong, I wasn't sure which, but their movements looked graceful and soothing. I had stopped meditating and was seeking something to calm my nervous system. I'm high-strung by nature, another trait I inherited from my mother. I started asking around and found a class for beginners in Tai Chi close to my neighborhood. I fell in love with the practice, which reminded me of how much I had loved to dance as a little girl. Moving my body in slow motion put me into ecstatic states.

After a year of practicing each day at home, I realized how much I had missed meditation. My Tai Chi instructor told me that Jack Kornfield, one of the preeminent teachers of Vipassana in our country, offered Monday night meditation classes in Marin County, a forty-five-minute drive each way.

It's not that therapy wasn't helping, it was. I was gaining more insight into my depression and my overall dissatisfaction with my life. But the silent movements of Tai Chi opened a need for a different kind of pathway into myself, the big Self often referred to as the Higher or True Self. Though it was a trek, I rearranged my schedule so that I could attend classes a few times a month. Jack was a master, and I wanted to learn from the best.

After attending Jack's Monday night meditation classes for a few years, I began to question the value of what I was doing as a therapist. Psychology, which is designed to strengthen the ego, felt at odds with the practice of emptying out the ego. In my practice of meditation, I was able to disidentify from my mind and momentarily experience freedom from my painful egoic history. And that was enabling me to go deeper in my work with Peter. I wondered if there was a way to take my psychotherapy with clients to this deeper level and still call it therapy.

One evening I approached Jack after class and shared my thoughts. I asked if he knew of any psychotherapists in the area who combined therapy with spiritual practice. Jack mentioned a name I was familiar with.

"I've met him and read his book. I don't think he's a fit for me. Do you know of anyone else?"

Jack looked down, taking his time before answering my question. When he looked up, he told me about a man named Hameed Ali, who was teaching something called the Diamond Approach. "I don't think he's accepting new students, but you might see if you can find a teacher who lives in Marin." By this time, I had sold my home in San Francisco and was renting a small cottage in San Anselmo.

"Funny you should mention him. The woman I see for acupuncture in San Francisco just gave me a flyer about a group Hameed is forming for psychotherapists. I don't know anything about the Diamond Approach, but I'll check it out."

I wondered about Jack's hesitancy in recommending Hameed and only later discovered, from a dedication in one of Jack's books, that Hameed was his teacher.

Once again, I felt the support of Divine Guidance pointing the way. I dug the flyer out from under a stack of papers on my desk as soon as I got home. The group was forming in February, so I had only a few weeks to apply. I picked up the book my acupuncturist, Karen, had recommended—*Diamond Heart Book I*—and read a chapter on the Theory of Holes. I was riveted. Hameed was describing a way to work with the inherent sense of deficiency that is the hallmark of the ego, a result of loss of contact with our essential nature during our formative years.

For example, if we're not allowed to be assertive, as was true for me with my domineering mother, we lose awareness of our innate strength. We can defend against the deficiency by being boisterous or aggressive. "I can do anything." Or we can go along with the deficiency, which I did, and believe that we can't do anything. We don't stand up for ourselves, have difficulties setting boundaries, and feel weak inside.

And here's the brilliant part of the theory, which I still consider one of the most profound teachings of the Diamond Approach. The way through the holes or deficiencies is to neither defend against or go along with them but counterintuitively go right into the deficiency: to feel into the painful and traumatic beliefs and emotions that make up our historical identity. Only when we can be with what is, even if what we feel in the moment is weakness, can we experience the emptiness that is at the center of any hole, emptiness being the fundamental nature of our consciousness. And in that emptiness, there lies the possibility of reconnecting with our essential strength. The same is true for whatever we believe we are "missing": power, joy, beauty, kindness, confidence, intelligence, and hundreds of other essential aspects and dimensions.

This was exactly what I was looking for, a path that used Western psychology and Eastern spiritual teachings to penetrate and free the ego. I had a strong hunch that this path could provide guidance for me in my work with clients, but also for myself. I longed to be free of the low self-esteem and lack of confidence that had plagued me for most of my life. My only hesitance was the name, Diamond Approach. It sounded New Age to me and lacked the heft of traditional Eastern paths that had been in existence for thousands of years.

I sent in my letter of application and was accepted within a week. Only later would I realize that everything I had studied prior to that moment had prepared me for this path: familiarity with psychological concepts, experience with body therapies, and five years of meditation practice.

CHAPTER THIRTEEN

Finding Home

In early February 1990, I attended my first weekend taught by Hameed. Seventy students, mostly psychotherapists, crowded into Hameed's basement meeting room in Berkeley. I didn't know anyone and, as was my habit, gravitated toward the back of the room, allowing for an easy escape if needed.

Promptly at 10:00 a.m., a short Middle Eastern man, a crutch under one arm, walked into the room and took a seat in front of the group. He placed the gold mala beads wrapped around his fingers onto the table next to him, welcomed us to the Therapists Group, and introduced the three female teachers who would be assisting with the teachings. Though he wasn't charismatic, as soon as Hameed began to speak, I was drawn in by his steady, deep presence.

"We'll start with the Kath meditation, a concentration practice which is a foundational practice of the Work. We focus on the Kath point, the center of Presence, located in the lower belly. We keep returning to it when our mind wanders, sensing the rising and falling of the abdomen as breath passes in and out of the body. Start by closing your eyes and resting your hands on your lap or on your belly. Don't try to find the Kath. Just keep bringing your awareness back to the belly. After we sit for twenty minutes, I'll ring the bell. There will be time for questions afterward."

And with that, Hameed rang a bell, and we sat. It sounded simple enough, but as with all meditation practices, this one was simple but not easy. My mind wandered here, there, and everywhere. Though we were told to notice the breath rising and falling, like Vipassana, the focus on the belly was different. I realized that I rarely noticed my belly other than to try to suck it in whenever I felt fat. Which was often despite my size 8 body. And forgetting Hameed's instructions, I tried desperately to find my Kath, having no idea what I was looking for.

Once Hameed began teaching, I had no difficulty being present. His words touched my psyche like soft raindrops on parched earth. The topic for the weekend was Love of Truth, which Hameed described as the fundamental orientation to the Work.

"We're not trying to get somewhere, or alleviate something difficult," he said. "Moving toward truth is a love affair, True Nature loving to reveal itself and our loving to behold its revelation and beauty."

Not trying to get somewhere? For an ambitious, task-driven personality like me, this sounded revolutionary. If there was a test to be taken, I had already failed during the Kath meditation. I wondered what that might be like to be simply curious about my experience, not pushing it in one direction or another. To feel my way, rather than direct it with a mind filled with notions of success or fitting in or being valued.

I had for years felt like a black sheep, both in my family and in the various professional choices I had made. Instead of studying Freudian analysis, I chose Transactional Analysis.

Instead of staying in the Northeast near my family, I moved three thousand miles away to California. Instead of Catholicism, I chose Buddhism. I didn't know it at the time, but each choice inched me closer to my true self and further away from conventional views of reality.

And now this, the Diamond Approach, an esoteric teaching that I knew little about but felt compelled to follow. The little I had read about it ignited a spark, a desire to go deeper, which I hadn't felt in a long time. I tried to avoid discovering the truth of my nature in my therapy sessions with Peter, fearing that I would discover something dark and hateful. In my Vipassana meditation practice, I tended to avoid investigating negative feelings by returning to my breath, a sort of transcendence rather than diving into what was arising.

As Hameed continued to teach, I wept quietly, knowing in my heart that I was in the right place. It would take years of practice to interrupt my habit of overadapting to what others expected of me, to learn how to be curious rather than judgmental about who I was and what I wanted. To trust my heart and let it guide my mind. It remains a practice, but in that moment, all I knew was that I had found a home.

A year after joining the group, I began working weekly with a private teacher, Jeanne Rosenblum. Three of my friends were seeing her, and I liked what they shared about how she worked. Direct, compassionate, and dedicated to the path. At my first session I felt my usual insecurity, wanting her to like me, trying to make a good impression. She indulged me for a few sessions while I told stories about myself, my history, how I was experiencing the teachings while avoiding being completely present and inquiring into my immediate experience.

I noticed a mat on the floor, next to our chairs that faced each other. I was familiar with breathwork from my Bioenergetics training and Reichian work with Peter and felt my usual hesitation to stop talking and just breathe. By the fourth session, Jeanne invited me to lie down on the mat with my knees up, taking breaths into my belly, chest, and then exhaling. *So far, so good.*

And then, instead of telling her what was happening, she directed me to stay close to my body sensations, any images that were arising, any emotions I was experiencing. No stories, just simple answers to the questions. A sensation of feeling helpless and powerless took over my consciousness. I felt tearful and scared and shared that with Jeanne.

"Stay with those feelings. There's no need to change anything. Just allow what's arising to be here," said Jeanne. Her voice was gentle, and I felt my resistance soften. Instead of trying to rise above the experience, my usual pattern, I kept breathing and sensing, allowing myself to feel helpless and powerless, and nothing bad happened. What a welcome surprise!

Private sessions were an opportunity to work with the main practice of the Diamond Approach, which is inquiry: staying open and curious about whatever you are experiencing to discover deeper states of consciousness. Similar to any spiritual practice, the more you do it, the more facile you become with truly staying open to whatever is arising.

I grew to look forward to my sessions with Jeanne, and felt more willing to reveal myself to her, as well as when I did inquiries with other students in our teaching sessions with Hameed. What was liberating for me, and still is, is that unlike psychotherapy, there's no agenda, no problem to be solved, and no ego to strengthen. In fact, the opposite happens by simply exploring whatever is arising in the moment. Early in my work, I'd begin an inquiry with a fixed idea about myself, usually one that was causing me great suffering, and end up feeling ecstatic as a hole opened to an essential aspect of True Nature. The path was a natural fit for me.

Two years into attending monthly weekend meetings, I was invited to participate in a teacher training program. Given my low self-esteem, I thought someone had made a mistake, an echo of being chosen queen of the junior prom in high school. I did not yet appreciate what I might have to offer as a teacher. But I trusted where I was being guided and faithfully showed up for weekly trainings and teaching retreats that took place over the next seven years.

Teacher training was an intense immersion into the intricate teachings of the Diamond Approach. Every Monday evening, my friend Sherry and I would drive from Marin County to Berkeley for a three-hour training session. Twice a year, we'd attend a five-day retreat, diving deeply into the same teachings I had been exposed to in my ongoing teachings with Hameed. This was in addition to a yearly ten-day summer retreat for all the students of the Diamond Approach. It was a huge commitment of time and money, but one that I felt completely committed to. In time, the teachings arose spontaneously in my consciousness. I was learning from my direct experience instead of relying on an outside authority to show the way. After seven years of training, which felt akin to getting a doctorate degree, I was ordained a teacher in December 1999.

Somewhere along the way, these teachings replaced religion and psychotherapy as my moral compass. Through meditation, inquiry, and practices of presence, I discovered deeper and deeper realms of Reality that transcended the black-and-white teachings of Catholicism I had grown up with.

Without being fully aware of the process, I not only became a teacher of the Diamond Approach but was shaped into a servant of the Divine, fulfilling the vision I had as a young girl. It ignited my desire to spend more time practicing meditation and ultimately led to my decision to spend a month at Gampo Abbey.

CHAPTER FOURTEEN

A New Perspective

The Diamond Approach had an impact not just on my personal perspective but on my professional one as well. My approach to psychotherapy was changing, too, and came to a head during a session with one of my favorite clients. Lori worked for a prominent San Francisco advertising firm, was divorced, and suffered from bouts of low self-esteem and depression. I think I saw in her a kindred spirit, a woman who was a dynamo professionally but thought of her personal life as a failure.

Though skeptical about therapy initially, Lori became a convert in the three years that we had been working together. In her office, she kept a postcard with the word *BREATHE* on it—a gift from me—and would pull it out and hold it up during meetings when things got charged.

"I tell my staff it's a tool from my therapist, and that I've paid her a lot of money for this advice so they should listen up." Lori had a sharp mind and great sense of humor.

One day, as Lori sat staring at the floor, her body slumped over, she said, "Some days I wonder what's the point of living. And don't tell me I have so much to be thankful for."

Lori owned a stunning home in Tiburon, overlooking the San Francisco Bay, and an enviable professional life.

"Well, how about instead we explore what the point of living might be. Maybe it's not what you think."

Since becoming a student of the Diamond Approach, I kept my spiritual explorations to myself, but something told me that Lori might be ready for more than the standard psychotherapeutic response to her question.

"What do you mean?" she asked.

"What if there's something more fundamental to living than who you are or how you were raised or how successful you are at work? Or where you live? Or who you're in a relationship with?"

Lori looked puzzled.

"I have no idea what you're talking about. I'm a what-you-see-is-what-you-get kind of gal," she said.

"Yup. I was pretty much like that myself until I began practicing meditation. It opened my mind to a whole new way of seeing life."

"You're not going to get all woo-woo on me, are you?"

I laughed. "I hope not. But do you remember when you first showed up for therapy? You didn't believe that talking about your history could help. Don't you feel better about yourself now than when we started working together?"

Lori nodded. "But I'm not a religious person. I left all of that behind when I moved here from the Midwest."

"I'm not talking about religion. I'm talking about our fundamental or True Nature. Not just the nature of human beings, but of all beings. Including your cats."

Lori nodded. "Sometimes, if I'm crying or depressed, they stare at me, like they know something I don't know."

"What do you imagine they're perceiving?"

Lori closed her eyes and was quiet for a moment.

"I'm picturing Cocoa. He's the wise one. Something like 'You are so much more than this sorrow. You're amazing! Now get over yourself and pet me.'"

We both laughed. I noticed that Lori had teared up.

"Something about that touches you," I said. "Can you say more?"

Lori took a breath. "I do get glimpses, now and then, of what I call my God-given gifts. I didn't make myself smart or witty or kind. Those things come naturally. But I forget about them when I feel like shit."

"That's exactly what I'm talking about! What you call your God-given gifts are part of your essential nature. And they're always here, regardless of whether you're having a good or bad day. It's easy to forget on days when you're feeling down, like today. It happens to everybody. Me too."

Lori's eyebrows shot up. "You're kidding. I can't imagine you ever having bad days."

"Of course I do, though I navigate them better since I started meditating."

Was I being too self-disclosing? Perhaps. But in that moment, I cared more about offering Lori a lifeline than hiding behind my therapist's screen.

Lori pointed over my shoulder. "I've noticed those beads on your table, behind the candle. Do they have anything to do with meditation?"

"They do. They're called self-remembering or mala beads. They remind me to take a few moments between sessions to practice mindfulness."

"Well, I don't think beads are my thing. They look too much like rosary beads. But I'd like to learn about meditation. Would that help with my depression?"

"It could. It trains the mind to concentrate on something besides our thoughts. You know, all those stories you tell yourself that keep you attached to suffering."

"What stories?"

"Like the story that you're the one who failed in the marriage. Or that it was your ex-husband's fault for not working on it."

"Wait," Lori said. "Those are opposites."

"Yes," I said, "but I've heard you say both at different times. And they both make you feel badly about yourself. It's not that one story is right and the other wrong—or even that both are wrong. It's that they each keep you going around and around in a circle of suffering."

"Huh," Lori said.

"Meditation doesn't take away the pain of loss or hurt. Those things are real. But it helps us to let go of our stories and our emotional reactions to life's ups and downs."

"That sounds cool."

"It is. But it takes practice."

"Can you teach me how to meditate?"

I thought for a moment before answering.

"I'd like to preserve our time together to continue doing what we're doing—exploring what's important in your life. But there are many wonderful meditation teachers in San Francisco and Marin. I'll give you a list of them next time we meet."

My bookcase overflowed with spiritual and psychological books. I stood up, walked over to it, and pulled out Jack Kornfield's *A Path with Heart: A Guide Through the Perils and Promises of Spiritual Life*, which I offered to Lori.

After she left, I picked up my mala and reflected on the session. As a result of my work in the Diamond Approach, particularly in teacher training, I was beginning to answer the question I had posed to Jack Kornfield in 1989, if it was possible to combine therapy and spiritual work.

Therapy is about healing and strengthening the personality. Spiritual work is about moving *beyond* the personality, either through transcendence or through transformation. As long as we're identified with the personality, we can't discover who and what we truly are. And we can't be free from the suffering that comes from holding on to our old worn-out stories.

In that moment, I started thinking that my days as a psychotherapist were numbered and my future as a full-time spiritual teacher was where I was headed.

CHAPTER FIFTEEN

Parenting

But who was I to be a spiritual leader? I didn't have great confidence in my own abilities. In fact, I was still haunted by memories of my mother's voice: "You think you're so great. If your friends knew you the way I do, you wouldn't have any."

I had been deeply scarred by my mother's and Al's abuse. Whether I recognized it as trauma at the time or not, I carried all the signs of it: freezing when someone raised their voice, dissociating when I felt backed into a corner, shutting down my anger and collapsing instead. They both tried to blame me for their behavior.

"Look what you made me do," my mother often said.

"You provoked me," said Al after he beat me up.

As a child, I assumed it was my fault that my mother hit me, if only because she was more abusive with me than either of my sisters. I confused standing up for myself with being provocative.

When I became a mother, I had no idea how to parent my son in a way that allowed him to develop his own personality and still set boundaries. All I knew was that I didn't want to be abusive the way my mother had been with me. Greg was bright, energetic, funny, athletic, and opinionated. He seemed to know what he wanted when he wanted it and had a self-assurance about him that I envied. He was so like his father, traits I admired in Al too.

I remember standing on the front lawn of our home with Greg in my arms. He was about eighteen months old, and I was teaching him colors. As I pointed to his dad's blue and white boat parked across the street, I said, "See Daddy's boat? What color is it?"

"It's red!" Greg exclaimed.

"Well, no, it's blue and white."

"No, it's red." And he was done with the lesson. Squirming to get free, he hopped on his plastic foot-powered motorcycle and took off down the slight incline in our front yard.

I carried the wounds of my upbringing into parenting him, resolving not to break his spirit the way my parents had tried to break mine. But I lacked a roadmap for how to discipline a child, and it didn't seem like anyone around me knew either. The strict guidelines of my parents' generation were being tossed out in the name of freedom. Greg, being strong-willed, needed a mother who could meet his will intelligently, perhaps like an Aikido master, stepping back but not retreating, coming forward with force but not destroying. I was not that mother.

My son relished pushing boundaries at home and in school. By the time Greg was in fifth grade, he was having epic power struggles with his teacher, who called weekly to complain about his behavior. He interrupted during lessons, asking questions that challenged the teacher. He joked around with other students, disrupting class. He doodled instead of writing down lessons. I didn't like the teacher, finding him rigid and arrogant at times, so I could see why Greg reacted the way he did. But I also wanted him to behave, something I myself wasn't very successful at making him do.

I blamed myself for divorcing his dad and taking him so far away from family and friends in New Jersey. I felt alone, not knowing whom to turn to for guidance. None of my friends in San Francisco had children of their own. I often collapsed in the face of Greg's insistence on getting his own way, feeling overwhelmed or exhausted and sometimes both.

In April of Greg's tenth year, while I was brushing my teeth and daydreaming, I noticed Greg standing in the doorway of our tiny wood-paneled bathroom, his skinny frame leaning against the doorjamb.

"I need a man around the house, Mom. Too many girls in this place." The woman with whom I owned the duplex, or two-flat as they're called in San Francisco, had recently fallen in love with a woman, and they were living together downstairs. And we had a female springer spaniel.

I was quiet for a moment, toothbrush mid-air.

"What do you suggest we do, Greg?"

"You could marry Paul. I bet he'd like that."

Paul was the man I had been dating for the last year. He and Greg got along well, but Paul had no more interest in becoming a stepfather than I had in remarrying. After a few moments I said, "I don't think I'm ready for another marriage."

Greg didn't miss a beat. "Well then, can I go live with Dad?"

Five years earlier, I had promised Al that if he let me take Greg to San Francisco, I'd let Greg return to New Jersey to live with him when he was older. I was imagining high school, if ever, not sixth grade. Greg was precocious for his age and pushing boundaries more than usual. He hung out with friends who were streetwise, and I had concerns about him entering adolescence in our neighborhood. The Haight, famous for the Summer of Love in 1967, had become more gentrified by the time we moved in. But just a few blocks down the street from our house, many of the shops still sold drug paraphernalia, and addicts littered the sidewalks, begging for money.

Al by this time had bought a beautiful home with a swimming pool in a neighborhood with plenty of kids who safely played in the street with none of the dangers of urban living. And he had recently proposed to a woman who would become his fourth wife. Though the marriage was short-lived, the expectation was that she would keep the home fires burning and watch over Greg while Al met with his psychotherapy clients a forty-five minute drive away. Greg and his dad were thrilled when I agreed to let him move to New Jersey at the end of the summer.

In early May 1985, just three months before Greg was scheduled to move back with his dad, my friend Betts arrived from New York for a visit. A single mother herself, she understood the stresses of being on call day and night. Betts had known Greg since he was a toddler. When she offered to stay with him for an evening of pizza and a video so that I could have an overnight with Paul at his apartment, I gratefully accepted.

Sunday morning my mother phoned the flat. Greg answered, and, after a few exchanges, she asked where I was.

"She's at Paul's."

"Oh, what's she doing there?" asked my mother.

"Sleeping."

"You tell your mother to call me immediately!"

Greg phoned me at Paul's and told me I was "in big trouble with Nana." Snuggled up with Paul on his couch, I dialed her number and barely got out "Hi, Mom" before she launched into a tirade.

"You should be ashamed of yourself. I swear, Rosanne, you're headed straight for hell." I stiffened with the lethal blow that followed. "Thank God Greg will be living with his dad soon. At least he has *one* responsible parent."

Paul was close enough to hear her end of the conversation and watch me go almost catatonic. After I hung up, he asked why I let her talk to me that way. His mother was a child psychiatrist, and his main complaint about her was that she was too reserved. My relationship with my mother baffled him. I whined and sometimes raged about her, convinced I was the innocent victim of a big, mean monster. But I kept coming back for more, my own participation in a drama lost on me.

This time, however, Paul's simple question broke through a blind spot in my consciousness. I finally understood what good friends, and a therapist or two, had been telling me for years. It was time to cut the cord. I was thirty-eight years old, living three thousand miles away from my mother, but acting as if I were still a powerless little girl living under her roof.

The next morning, I phoned my mother from my kitchen. When she heard my voice on the line, she wasted no time. "You should be ashamed of yourself."

I cut her off.

"I have something to say, and I want you to listen without interrupting me."

I felt clear, calm, and fierce.

"If you ever speak to me that way again, I will cut you out of my life. You don't have to agree with my lifestyle or my values. But you need to treat me with respect. Talk to me the same way you talk to your friends, pretend to agree even when you don't. You can complain to Dad behind my back. But do not ever again attack me for who I am or how I'm living my life."

I paused only enough to take a breath, not wanting to give her an opening to react.

"I'm going to hang up now and give you the week to think. I'll phone you next Sunday just like I always do. If you agree to my terms, we don't have to discuss this again. We can just talk like normal. If you don't agree, hang up when you hear my voice. Understood?"

I didn't wait for an answer before placing the receiver of the bright red wall phone back in its cradle. The kitchen seemed brighter than usual as the morning sun streamed in the back windows. Crystal clarity everywhere my eyes landed. *I did it. I stood up to my mother!* I had taken the first step away from our enmeshed relationship. Walking, no, actually skipping, I made my way down the long hallway of the flat, passing through the dining room and living room, twirling in circles until I was at Greg's bedroom door. Time to wake him for school.

The following Sunday, true to my word, I phoned my parents. Mom answered sounding somewhat reserved. But she didn't hang up and didn't mention our last conversation. Nor did I. Over the next few months, we charted new territory, finding ways to relate more as equals.

During Greg's last spring and summer living with me, I was training to run the San Francisco marathon. I had run a few half-marathons and couldn't resist the challenge of running one of the most iconic races in the country. For 26.2 miles, runners traverse the hills and flats of the city, through Golden Gate Park, into the Presidio with its breathtaking views of the Golden Gate Bridge, along Aquatic Park and the Embarcadero, ending near City Hall. I had walked Mission Street several times but had never noticed its elevation until I was running my last four miles. A fellow runner saw me dragging and offered words of encouragement, which pulled me to the finish.

My only goal was to cross the finish line with a smile, which I did after four hours and twenty minutes. Paul and Greg joined me for a quarter of a mile as I climbed Fort Hill and were both there at the finish line, cheering me on. Afterward, I felt a quiet pride and satisfaction not unlike the way I felt after giving birth to Greg. Both were watershed moments that offered me a glimpse into my inner strength and fortitude; what looked like rebellion to my parents was the solidity of my own nature.

After the high of running the marathon, it was time to focus on preparing Greg for his move. I started marking events: last parent-teacher conference, last visit to Malibu Grand Prix raceway for kids in Redwood City, one last visit to Lake Tahoe with Paul. I couldn't resist buying the fancy leather gloves that Greg spotted at a ski shop end-of-season sale. As the blond twenty-something salesman crooned seductively, "Too cool for school. Too rad for Mom and Dad," I rationalized the cost, knowing he'd ski plenty next winter with his dad, who was on Ski Patrol.

As the time grew closer for Greg's departure, our power struggles intensified. We argued about homework and picking up his room and his newly acquired sullen attitude. We weren't just dealing with the impending physical separation. Greg was approaching adolescence and trying to assert his independence from me. But aside from my recent confrontation with my mother, I had no clue how to navigate this terrain. Instead, I acted like I had as a child with my mother. I got angry, provoked fights, and stomped off in silence to my bedroom. Sometimes I would collapse into the victim mentality, feeling powerless to assert boundaries, and then internally blame Greg for my helplessness.

It seemed nearly impossible to talk with Greg about what was happening, and instead I did what my mother did when she wanted to make up without having to apologize, which was to cook my favorite meal. Greg's was hot dogs and mac and cheese, and I made a lot of it during those last few months. I hated acting like my mother, but what I hated even more was feeling as powerless as I had as a child.

We went through his clothes and toys, picking out which ones to pack and which to leave behind for when he spent summers with me in San Francisco. I had pictured the day, the moment of saying goodbye, as a tender one. I would tell him how much I loved him, how I'd miss having him around, how dear to me he was and always would be.

Instead, we got into a fight at the airport about his backpack, which was stuffed so full he couldn't zip it closed. We were on the moveable walkway, approaching Greg's departure gate. He was in front of me, ignoring me as I called his name.

Hurrying to catch up, I shouted, "Greg, slow down. Your backpack's not zipped."

He turned to shoot me a look of disgust, saying "It's fine," before picking up his pace.

I wanted to scream at him and grab him by that half-zipped backpack and remind him that I was still his mother. When I finally caught up to him at the gate, I stood behind him, counting to ten to stop myself from escalating. *So what if something falls out of his bag?*

Greg kept his back to me until it was time to board his plane, giving me enough space to feel the grief that my outrage was covering up. When he turned, my eyes were wet. His face softened and he reached out to hug me. We embraced.

"I love you, Greg."

"I love you too, Mom."

And then he was gone.

CHAPTER SIXTEEN

More Letting Go

After Greg moved to New Jersey in 1986, I thought that the time alone would allow me to fill my empty tanks and resume a meditation practice. Instead, I dropped into a profound depression and barely had the energy to see my psychotherapy clients. I missed my son and wished I'd pulled him back into my arms before he boarded the plane that would set both of our lives on a different course.

Mike was growing increasingly alarmed at my unwillingness to talk about my feelings with him. Sharing our deepest emotions had been the foundation of our relationship. When I canceled a trip to Boston to do a Transactional Analysis treatment weekend with his clients on the Cape, something we took turns doing with Mike's clients back East and mine in California, he confronted me about not caring about my life.

He was right. Living didn't feel like a viable option, nor did dying. I wasn't suicidal, but I'd lost my zest for life and my nerve for tolerating painful emotions. I convinced myself that I could go through the motions of living until I died. I didn't want to be alone, but wanted to be left alone, a confusing, immobilizing state. The only time I felt a sense of purpose was when I was working with clients.

Mike and I argued more during our phone conversations, him trying to help by suggesting I try a different therapist or end the relationship with Paul. I didn't want advice. I wanted him to understand but not push me to be any other way than how I was.

The next time Mike visited me in San Francisco, we were hanging out in his hotel room, lying on the bed, smoking a joint.

"Whatever possessed you to move across the country for a man like Bob?" he asked.

"You abandoned me, remember, when you moved to Boston with Ginny," I answered before realizing I was opening Pandora's box. We had swept that one under the carpet, and now it was back.

"What do you mean, 'I abandoned you'?"

"When I rented that house in Peapack after my divorce, you promised you'd help me with Greg and then you were gone."

"But I didn't abandon you," he said. "I stayed in touch and visited you in New Jersey and you visited me in Boston."

"You broke my heart, Mike, when you chose Ginny."

Mike jumped up off the bed, clearly angry.

"You make it sound like moving to Boston was some kind of marriage proposal. I'm *gay*," he shouted, "and I'll always be gay. You've never accepted that."

"That's not true," I shouted back, even though he was right. "You're the one who's made it hard for me to move on. Be honest. Have you ever liked any man I've been with?"

"No. But that's because you have such poor taste in men."

I turned on my heels and left, slamming the door behind me.

We stopped talking to each other, or more accurately Mike stopped returning my calls. He sent a letter, saying he needed some space to think about our relationship. I wrote a few times, but never heard back from him. It was now the second time in my life that someone I loved had disowned me. First my mother when I married Al, and now my soulmate. How had my personal life turned into such a mess?

In January 1986, I sold my flat in the Upper Haight, and Paul, his friend, and I bought a three-story building together in the Richmond area of San Francisco. We occupied the third floor, with a view of the ocean off Baker Beach. Paul's friend lived on the second floor, and we rented out the ground-level apartment to help finance the mortgage.

"Don't expect me to visit you while you're living in sin," Mom said during the phone conversation when I told her of my plans. Had she said something like this in the past, we would have gotten into an ugly argument. But things had changed since I had finally stood up to her six months earlier. Instead, I said, "I understand."

Within a year of moving in with Paul, and after sending photos of our new place, Mom and Dad were on a plane to San Francisco. They never could resist the lure of their favorite city. They stayed with Paul and me, and it was the first time I felt like an adult in their presence. We had an enjoyable time cooking together, visiting some of our favorite tourist spots, and introducing them to restaurants in our neighborhood. Absent was any further conversations about me living in sin.

But I was not happy. I missed Mike, I missed my son, and I had concerns about how his dad was parenting him. And I was burning out on psychotherapy. I started contemplating going back to graduate school for a PhD in organizational psychology, imagining that it would be less stressful than working with clients. Researching schools gave me a boost for a few months, but when it came time to send in applications, I lost interest. It wasn't the answer.

Nor was Paul. Early in 1989, I met with the psychic that both Mike and I had worked with over the years. Joya was visiting San Francisco, and we agreed to meet at a coffee shop near her hotel. She worked with photos, and I arrived with my stack. Within moments, the table was a chaotic mess of purse, hat, and a bag of books that Joya had just purchased. She pulled a small crystal out of her purse, cleared a space, and set it in the middle of the table with one hand while signaling the waitress with another. Coffee drinks on the way, we set about the task of my reading. I pulled out my photos and placed them next to the crystal. Over cappuccinos, she studied them. I told her about my estrangement from Mike and Greg's move to New Jersey and my concerns about whether I should bring him back to San Francisco.

With a wave of her hand, she let me know she'd heard enough. She started with Mike.

"I know it's painful for you right now, but you're soulmates. You'll find your way back to each other eventually."

Next, she picked up the photos of Greg and his dad. "It's their karmic destiny to be together right now. Which doesn't mean it's all going well or will go well in the future, but your son is where he needs to be. It's better that you not interfere in that relationship."

I was getting ready to plead my case when Joya cut me off. "You survived your mother. He'll survive his father." Though it was true that I had survived, I was left with the hidden wounds of trauma in my psyche, and it was taking a lot of personal work for me to thrive. I didn't want Greg to suffer the same fate, yet there was some wisdom to what Joya was saying. Greg and Al had a close relationship, and neither of them were interested in him moving back with me. I needed to sit back and let things play out, assuring myself that, if necessary, I could take action.

Lastly, she studied the photos of Paul.

"Well, you don't need to ask me any questions about him. Paul is a lovely man with a good heart, and he cares for you. But you need to get out of the way. His life partner is about to show up, and the two of them will have a child together. He's too nice to leave you, so you'll have to leave him, but it will all work out in the end."

"What about me? Do I have a life partner showing up too?"

"That's not so clear," Joya said. "What is clear is that you need to end the relationship with Paul and see what happens next."

When I shared the reading with Paul that evening over dinner, I was taken aback when he smiled broadly.

"Wow, you don't seem surprised. Have you met her already?" I asked.

"No. But our relationship has been the longest one of my life. I think I'm finally ready to marry and start a family. It just hasn't quite clicked for us."

After Paul and I separated a few months later, I felt broken and wondered if I was incapable of having a successful relationship. True to Joya's prediction, Paul met his life partner within a year, and he and Carol married and had a child together.

I gave passing thought to joining a monastery, a fantasy I returned to over and over when I wondered if I'd lost my way.

CHAPTER SEVENTEEN

The Earth Moves

On October 17, 1989, the largest earthquake to hit the Bay Area since 1906 shook the ground with a vengeance. I was in my office on Union Street with a client when we felt the jolt. It sounded like someone had hit the building with a cannon ball, a loud bang, and then the lights went out. We stared at each other for a moment, trying to comprehend what was happening, and then said simultaneously, "Earthquake!"

Pulling open the sliding doors, we stood in the doorframe waiting for the next shock. But that was the end of it, no swaying or rumbling, just silence. It was still light outside at 5:00 p.m., and we were in the middle of our session, so we both sat down to continue.

But within minutes, we heard sirens and voices out on the street just below my window. I opened it, and we both stuck our heads out to see what was happening. A few men were standing by a parked car with its doors open, listening to the news.

"What's going on?" I shouted to them.

"There's been a big earthquake, down the Peninsula. Buildings collapsed in the Marina. And they've stopped the baseball game."

I went from feeling on high alert to terrified. The Marina district, just a few blocks down from Union Street, was built almost entirely on landfill and the ground had turned to mush. The "game" he was referring to was the first game of the World Series being played between our two local teams, the San Francisco Giants and the Oakland Athletics.

"Is it safe to stay inside?" I called to one of the men.

"I don't think so. They're saying something about a collapse on the Bay Bridge."

As sirens wailed, my client and I vacated the building quickly and went our separate ways. In my panic, I couldn't remember where I parked my car and wandered up and down a few streets until I found it. Residents were gathering in clusters outside their apartments, taking comfort in human contact. The ten-minute drive out to the avenues stretched into half an hour. I avoided my usual route along the Marina and instead snaked my way through the steep streets of Pacific Heights until I found an entrance to Golden Gate Park. By the time I exited the park, an eerie silence had descended on the normally bustling city. The streets were empty, and the news on the radio was sketchy but frightening. I wondered if I'd even have a home to return to.

To my great relief, my neighborhood seemed unaffected. Until I learned later that the area was built on bedrock, I feared that at any minute, the house might collapse during an aftershock. I parked the car on the street, afraid to drive into the garage. Before entering, I checked the foundation, which had a small crack but otherwise looked solid. Inside the house, there were some minor cracks in the wall leading up the stairwell. My upright piano had rolled across the foyer and was wedged against the banister, which had stopped it from tumbling down the three flights of stairs.

I headed to the bedroom. I wasn't hungry and couldn't watch the news on TV because nobody in the city had power. I gathered whatever candles I could find, plus a large flashlight, and crawled under the covers. The phone wasn't dead, but I couldn't get an outside line. I knew my parents would be worried, that they would be trying to contact me. That emergency preparedness kit was still on a to-do list. Did I have enough water? Canned food? How long could I survive without power?

The sound of a ringing phone interrupted my thoughts. I jumped out of bed and grabbed the receiver.

"Rose, thank God you're there!" It was the familiar deep voice of Mike, whom I hadn't spoken to in three years. I started sobbing and couldn't answer.

"Talk to me. Are you OK?" he asked.

"Yes, yes, I'm just scared and so relieved to hear your voice. I couldn't get an outside line and there's no power. I have no idea what's happening."

I could hear Mike's television in the background as he slowly described what he was seeing. A section of the Bay Bridge had collapsed, as well as an overpass leading to the bridge. Cars were crushed under the rubble, and several people had died. If it hadn't been for the World Series game, there would have been many more fatalities. The quake struck at 5:04, the height of rush hour traffic, but many of the usual commuters were standing safely in the stadium listening to the national anthem. Mike described the fires in the Marina, many of the structures in rubble, power outages throughout the Bay Area. This is "the big one," the newscasters were saying, the one we all lived in fear of but, like death, didn't think would happen to us.

Back under the covers, I asked Mike to call my parents and Greg. And then I made him promise that he would never stop talking to me again.

Mike's response was perfect. "We have so much to catch up on. I can't even remember what we argued about. All I know is that I want you back in my life."

"Me, too, you," I said. "And your timing is impeccable! I'll never forget that you were the first person I talked to."

After we hung up, I felt a wave of relief. Our estrangement was over, and I knew, even if there was some awkwardness, we'd found our way back to each other as Joya had predicted. What that would look like was still unknown, but I took comfort in our reconciliation.

Soon after the earthquake, one of the psychologists from the upstairs office stopped by to tell me that he was closing his practice and taking a sabbatical for three months. Rich and I had spoken casually on a few occasions, and I liked him but knew little about him. I offered to treat him to a goodbye lunch, and the next week, over Caesar salads and coffee, sparks started flying. He was easy to talk to, intelligent with a wry sense of humor. And his eyes, oh my! Dark and mysterious, and when he looked intently at me as I spoke, my stomach flipped.

It would be many years before I realized how much Rich resembled Mike. People often compared the two to Tom Selleck: Mike was a grayer version and Rich's hair still black back then. Mike had blue eyes, Rich's were dark brown, and their personalities were so different that I missed the obvious. Not until Rich began graying did I realize with some embarrassment that the initial attraction, at least in looks, was a straight version of Mike.

The last thing I needed, though, was another relationship. I'd put off my spiritual pursuits long enough and, only slightly tongue in cheek, told Rich that I was headed for a monastery. He was hoping to remarry and have children. As we walked back to our offices, he asked if he could phone me when he was in town to visit his sister in Berkeley. We exchanged home phone numbers and hugged goodbye just outside my office. I liked the feel of his body against mine. *Maybe a little fling before I enter the monastery.*

In late October, Rich phoned from Ashland, Oregon, a stop he'd made on his way up the Pacific coast. After he filled me in on how his sabbatical was going, which had included a backpacking trip in the Sierras, he suggested that I join him in Ashland the following weekend to see some plays.

It was tempting, but I had already signed up for a retreat in Watsonville with Jack Kornfield and I didn't want to miss it. Rich ended the call with "maybe another time."

I wasn't sure if he'd call again and when he did, I was excited to hear his voice. He was passing through the Bay Area to tie up some loose ends with his former psychology partner and wondered if we could get together.

I swear God was testing me on my resolve to make spiritual life my priority! I had tickets to see the Dalai Lama, a sold-out function, and it wasn't an option for me to miss sitting with this holy man in person.

"I'm so sorry, but I can't. I have tickets to see the Dalai Lama. Our dates aren't meshing, but I really do hope you'll try again."

"I will," he promised.

True to his word, Rich phoned in November to say that he had accepted a psychology position in Salt Lake City and would be moving in December. He wanted to visit his sister before his move and wondered if we could meet on November 12, the same weekend I had tickets to see Pat Rodegast, a woman who channeled Emmanuel. I'd read her book, *A Manual for Living Comfortably in the Cosmos,* and had sat with her the last time she was in San Francisco.

When I mentioned this to Rich, he was quiet for a moment and then said, "I've asked three times and won't ask again. Sounds like you've got a busy life."

I liked his forthrightness. *A man who speaks his mind.* And I wasn't ready to pass up an opportunity to check out our attraction to each other. I told him I knew of someone who'd love the ticket, and we made a date.

The plan was to meet at my flat and have dinner at one of the Chinese restaurants in my neighborhood. Since Rich would be arriving while I was still at the office, I told him where to find a key and invited him to make himself at home and hang out with the cats until I showed up.

When I arrived, he greeted me at the top of the stairs, and, within seconds, we were passionately kissing as if already lovers. Catching my breath, I pulled back to look at him. Neither of us said a word, and then we simultaneously burst out laughing. Taking his hand, I led him down the hallway into the kitchen, pulled a bottle of chardonnay from the fridge, and gave him a tour of the house. On the way to the living room, my two cats circled our feet. They joined us on the couch as we sipped wine and caught up with each other.

Hours passed like minutes and when we noticed we were hungry, it was close to 8:00. Neither of us felt like breaking the intimacy of the moment by sitting in a restaurant, so I offered to pull something together. Pickings were slim. I opened a can of clams, doctored them up with fresh parsley, garlic, and Parmesan cheese, and served them over linguini. Hardly haute cuisine, but it hit the spot. After we finished eating and the dishes were soaking in the sink, things got awkward. *Will he stay or drive to his sister's? If he stays, will he sleep in the guest room or share my bed?*

Standing in the hallway, the scene of our first passionate kiss, we decided to put off the decision and instead take a walk on Baker Beach. It was a typical fall night in the city, cool and clear, the stars filling the black sky. We had the beach to ourselves and silently strolled hand in hand near the water's edge. The air was refreshing, stimulating our senses, and by the time we were back at the flat, the choice of where he would sleep was obvious. We tumbled into my bed, hands groping here and there, clothes flying in all directions. He ended up staying for the weekend.

I was slightly chagrined at my behavior. I had vowed to be alone, and here I was starting an affair. When Mike called a few days later and I told him about my tryst, he put words to my misgivings.

"Please don't jump into another relationship! Give yourself some time to breathe."

When we parted after that weekend, Rich and I planned a rendezvous in January in Salt Lake. Our lives were moving in different directions, and neither of us thought of this as a potential long-term relationship. He was looking for a young woman to bear his children, and I was pursuing my spiritual life. Having given myself up first to my mother, and then to boyfriends and husbands, I was determined to give myself over to myself.

But as Tom Robbins of *Even Cowgirls Get the Blues* fame said, "Plans are one thing, fate another."

CHAPTER EIGHTEEN

Togetherness

After two years of dating, Rich and I decided to buy a house together. It was a challenging process, since we had different ideas of how to make the decision. We both had controlling parents and liked being the one calling the shots. Compromising felt too much like being dominated, and neither of us could tolerate that.

I knew from the experience of buying and selling three homes that when you find the house you love, you put in an offer. Given my impulsive nature, I was comfortable acting quickly. Rich preferred to ponder, to consider all the options. This was his first house, and he wanted to get it right.

We started going to open houses and meeting realtors who were eager to sell given low inventory. At one of the open houses, we met a realtor we both liked and described our ideal house. Three bedrooms, two baths, traditional rather than modern, with an updated kitchen and nice garden area. We preferred the town of San Anselmo because of its many treed lots and charming downtown area. The realtor found it within a week, and we both liked it. But Rich wanted more time to look at other houses. The more I pushed for a quick decision, the more Rich dug in his heels. By the time he was ready, the house had sold.

We looked at many more houses and ended up buying one that neither of us was crazy about other than its location and "good bones," as the realtor was fond of repeating each time we hesitated. It turned out to be a good enough home. As we went through rounds of renovations, making it our own, we came to lovingly refer to it as our teacher. It taught us how to work our differences to our advantage, me seeing the big picture but missing important details while Rich took the time to ensure that we were making good choices.

About six months after moving into our house, standing in the kitchen after a long day of work, I got impatient with Rich. I was hungry and eager to dig into our takeout pizza.

"Hurry up. The pizza's getting cold," I said.

"It can wait. I need to make a quick phone call before we eat."

I hated feeling controlled and he hated being pushed, but, in that moment, all I could think about was myself.

"Why can't you just eat now and make the call later?"

Rich glared at me as he banged his plate down on the counter. He turned on his heels and headed for the bedroom. When I heard the door slam shut, I took my plate and threw it against the wall, then stomped out of the house.

It was dark, and I was crying, feeling helpless and trapped. *I hate him, I hate him,* I said out loud to an empty neighborhood. Drapes were closed, and I imagined happy couples sitting inside, watching television, enjoying pleasant conversation at the end of a long day.

I chastised myself. *Why did you ever agree to live with someone again? This always happens, you're better off alone.* I repeated my mantra. *I hate him. I hate him.* I thought about Al and how he tried to squash me. I thought about Bob and how clingy he was. I felt a familiar tight knot in the middle of my chest.

I thought about Rich, but he didn't fit into either of those categories. Yes, he was a perfectionist at times and yes, he liked to have things his way, but so did I. He was also kind and willing to talk things through with me when we had disagreements. As I reflected on his many positive traits—trustworthy, reliable, bright, funny—it dawned on me that he was the best man I'd ever hated.

As I continued to walk, a deeply embedded pattern revealed itself. I'd fall easily in love, idealizing whomever I was with. Eventually, as happens in any relationship, the other person would say or do something hurtful or upsetting, bursting my love bubble. Rather than address the issue, I'd suppress my feelings. Anything to avoid turning into a raging maniac like my mother. Instead, I'd blame myself, much like I did as a child, and seethe with hatred, for myself and the other. Eventually I'd run out of storage space for all the unexpressed resentments and start planning my exit strategy. The idea of confronting problems head-on seemed impossible. It never worked with Mom, so why would I expect it to work with anyone else?

And then I heard Hameed's words in my head saying something about hatred. *What was it he said? That it was a barrier to Peace and Power?* I felt anything but peaceful or powerful in that moment. I remembered him calling this essential aspect Black, because of its qualities of a deep, dark stillness in the soul when we are at peace, when the usual agitation of the mind quiets down and we drop into the depth of our being.

My pace slowed down as I tried to recall more details about the Black and hatred. I hated so many people in my life, starting with my mother. Because I was terrified of being domineering like her, I squelched my personal power. Hameed had said that, as a first step in accessing true power and peace, we needed to acknowledge and feel into our hatred, not easy for a Catholic girl who grew up thinking hatred was a sin. That's when I realized that I was *experiencing* my hatred rather than rejecting or judging it. It brought a sense of elation, liberation, and I couldn't wait to go home and make peace with Rich. I didn't want to leave yet another man, and I didn't want to keep running from myself, from my hatred and sense of powerlessness. I'd met my match, someone willing to spar with me without overpowering me.

When I walked in the front door, the house seemed particularly still. Had Rich left, or was the peace of the Black permeating not only me but space everywhere? I paused, taking in the stillness. I looked down the hallway and saw that the bedroom door was still shut. Before sharing my insights with Rich, I decided to first clean up the mess I'd made when I threw the dish against the wall. I picked up the broken plate in the dining room but couldn't find the piece of pizza. I walked in circles in the kitchen and dining room before giving up the search and heading to the bedroom through the living room.

And there, sitting upside down on the fireplace hearth, was the sad piece of pizza. It must have ricocheted into the living room when the plate hit the wall. Pizza sauce formed an arc over Rich's expensive stereo equipment. I panicked. He took meticulous care of his possessions, especially anything to do with music. I wiped the sauce off the wall, carefully examined the tuner, and let out an audible exhale when I was certain that it had been spared my fury.

I walked down the hall and knocked on the door.

"Can I come in?" I asked.

Rich grumbled a yes, and I slowly opened the door. He was lying on the bed, looking angry and unwilling to make eye contact.

"I'm sorry for getting into a stupid argument with you. Can we talk about it?"

"I don't feel like it."

I got why he was angry and why he might, in that moment, hate me as much as I had hated him a few moments ago. Hating the one you love is not the opposite of loving the one you love, another realization I'd had as I was walking.

"I understand and I really do want to apologize. Not just for my part in our argument, but for all the times I've gotten defensive with you or shut down instead of listening."

Rich looked at me for the first time since I'd entered the bedroom. I took it as a sign to continue.

"It may sound crazy, but I had this realization while I was walking that made me very happy. You're the best man I've ever hated!" I was grinning broadly and watched Rich's expression change from anger to puzzlement.

"What about hating me makes you happy? That doesn't feel so good to me."

I shared more about my realization and how I knew I'd hurt him each time I threatened to leave him when I was feeling hurt and powerless, and that I wanted to stay this time with him.

"I hope you can forgive me and work with me on this one."

I told him that hatred and rejection were deeply embedded patterns, but now that I was aware of them, I was hopeful that they wouldn't ruin my relationships like they had in the past.

Rich was quiet, taking in what I shared and processing his own feelings. After a long pause, he spoke.

"You've made it hard for me to trust that you aren't going to walk out each time I express my anger."

"You're right. I'm not good with anger. But I want to learn how to stay and not run from myself or you."

We kept talking and eventually made peace with each other. And though there were more power struggles to come, knowing we could work through them gave me the courage to consider another marriage.

On October 2, 1994, Rich and I got married in the backyard of our home in San Rafael. Third time was the charm. We had waited five years before committing to marriage, not wanting to experience the humiliation of another failed one. Rich, too, had been married twice before and was as cautious as me. As a Sagittarius, I am by nature an optimist and was ready to make our commitment public.

The night before the wedding, Rich and I hosted a rehearsal dinner at our favorite Italian restaurant in downtown San Rafael. Both sets of parents arrived in the afternoon, along with Rich's sister. My parents stayed in our guest room, and Rich's parents and sister stayed in a nearby hotel. Rich's good friend from California and his wife showed up at the house about the same time as our families were meeting each other. It was chaotic. Mom kept asking me to check her outfit and make sure she looked OK. She was nervous, meeting Rich's parents, but her need for attention was driving me crazy. I was hoping for a time-out before my private Diamond Approach teacher, Jeanne, who would be officiating our wedding, arrived to walk us through the ceremony.

I grabbed Rich, and we drove to the top of the hill above our house. Sitting in the car looking out over the San Francisco Bay, we admitted that we were both feeling anxious. We wondered if we should have kept it simple, gone to City Hall and been married in private. It was a clear night. We held hands, taking in the beauty of the sunset, as we gathered ourselves before returning to the house.

When we walked in the front door, Jeanne greeted us and could tell by the look on my face that I was in a state. She'd heard plenty of tales of my mom in our private sessions, and she also knew my tendency to leave my center when I felt overwhelmed. Wisely, she invited Rich and me to come out to the patio, telling our guests that the rehearsal would start after the three of us had a chance to talk together. We sat at a small table with our printed-out ceremony before us. Jeanne put the papers aside and turned to me.

"Rose, do you want to marry Rich?" she asked.

"Yes," I said emphatically. "But my mom is already getting on my nerves, and I'm sorry we invited them to stay with us."

"I'm not surprised," Jeanne said. "She'll settle down once things get underway." Then she turned toward Rich.

"Rich, do you want to marry Rose?"

"Yes, I do," he said. "And I'll be relieved when the ceremony is behind us."

Jeanne took our hands and joined them on the tabletop.

"Please, enjoy every moment. This is a special time for both of you and a time to practice staying present." With a squeeze of our hands, she added, "I now pronounce you man and wife. Nothing more to do but enjoy the festivities."

Rich and I looked at each other and then burst out laughing. Our anxiety dropped away as we walked through the ceremony with Jeanne and our families before heading to the restaurant.

The weather was on our side the next day. We'd yet to start renovating our house, with its chartreuse siding and gray cement patio. The best you could say about the garden was that it had potential. We spruced it up with an altar that held photos of our grandmothers, a Buddha, and a huge floral arrangement from Mike and Moe.

Mike chose not to attend the wedding, saying he and Moe couldn't afford either the expense or time off from work to travel from Boston to California, having just attended a family reunion in Northern California in July. I didn't buy it. By now he'd met Rich a few times and remained ambivalent, much as he had about any of my love relationships. I was reluctant to confront him, not wanting to poke the bear. We'd been reconciled for five years, but I still didn't trust his willingness to stay friends through thick and thin. We were twin souls, after all, and I knew his propensity as well as I knew my own to bolt in the face of conflict.

I wore a white softly pleated mid-calf length dress, once again no veil. I splurged on a white silk shawl held in place by the "lucky pin," an 18-karat gold brooch with a large emerald, surrounded by diamonds and pearls. It was a Hunt family heirloom worn by Rich's maternal grandmother and mother at their weddings. His mother, Joyce, loaned it to me for my "something old," making sure I knew it was to be returned after the festivities. She reluctantly accepted me into the family, having hoped for grandchildren. I was Rich's third wife and Joyce's third daughter-in-law, so her reticence was understandable.

My parents, especially my mother, adored Rich. "Don't mess this one up," she told me after meeting him for the first time. Their only complaint was my refusal to take Rich's last name, Hunt. I was tired of taking other men's names, first Lawson, then Andersen. After months of contemplation, I chose instead my Nonna's last name, Annoni. My parents balked at this decision and addressed all future correspondence to me as Rosanne Hunt. Sometimes they'd include my first husband's last name, Rosanne Lawson Hunt, but never ever was I addressed as Rosanne Annoni.

After the ceremony, my father made a toast and welcomed Rich into our family, adding, "I hope you have better luck controlling her than we did." A photo caught my mother laughing and playfully hitting my dad, while I sat on his other side, stunned.

Rich's sister jumped up from her seat to welcome me into the Hunt family, and to let my parents know that she considered my feistiness an asset. "I come from a long line of strong women. Any woman who can throw a piece of pizza at my brother is most welcomed into this family." I deeply appreciated her acceptance of me just as I was.

We drank champagne and feasted on poached salmon and wedding cake. After the guests left, we sat in our living room with our families and a few close friends. Though we had been together for five years, I felt different, *married*. I got it this time: for better or worse, in hatred and love.

CHAPTER NINETEEN

Approaching Forgiveness

Although I experienced increasing degrees of autonomy from my mother, imprints of our difficult relationship remained, offering plenty of fodder for me to work with over the years. Just before traveling to Allentown in 1996 for a visit with my parents, I met with my Diamond Approach teacher, Jeanne, for a private session. My sisters hoped that I could persuade our parents, who were now in their mid-eighties, to sell their three-story home and move into an independent living community. "Mom listens to you," my older sister said.

Sitting across from Jeanne in her home office, I took a few moments to sense myself—emotions, body tensions, thoughts—and then told her I was anxious about the visit. Things were better between Mom and me, but it still took a lot of effort for me to stay centered around her if I was in her company for more than two days.

Jeanne was listening carefully, as if she hadn't heard me complain about my mother a hundred times before.

"All my years of therapy and sitting meditation help," I said. "But no matter what, after a few days I want to strangle her."

"And right now?" Jeanne asked. "How do you feel as you talk about your mother?"

"Truthfully? I feel young and insecure. I'm so confident and grown up when I'm sitting with my therapy clients or my students, but put me in a room with her and I regress. I hate it."

"What's the 'it' that you hate?"

I pondered the question. On first impulse, I wanted to say "her," but that didn't feel true. *What do I hate?*

And then it came, and I knew it was the truth because my eyes filled with hot tears.

"I hate myself for taking the bait. For screaming at her. For acting like a child. I should know better by now."

Jeanne invited me to take a few breaths and sense again what I was feeling. Not just emotionally but including the entirety of my physical presence. We were both quiet for several minutes while I sensed and breathed. In time, I became aware of a dull ache in my chest, as if there were a black pebble lodged in the middle of my heart. It was a familiar sensation, but one I hadn't yet explored.

"Focus on the pebble," said Jeanne, "taking gentle breaths into it. How big is it?"

"About the size of a kalamata olive. It's hard and cold and I want to rip it out."

"Is it possible to be curious about it instead? Perhaps we can see what this hard pebble is doing in your heart rather than trying to get rid of it."

I didn't want to. But if I'd learned anything from the Diamond Approach and Hameed, a fan of *Star Trek*, it was that *resistance is futile.* I took more breaths into the pebble and noticed that the space around it was warm and open, which I shared with Jeanne.

When Jeanne asked if the pebble had anything it wanted to say, I was surprised at how quickly the answer came.

Stop rejecting yourself for what you feel.

The pebble softened.

"I so wish I was over hating my mother and hating myself for hating her."

Jeanne reminded me that a basic tenet of most spiritual practices is to be fully present with things as they are. As I allowed myself to feel my gnarly feelings toward myself and my mother, I relaxed. The spacious warmth that was surrounding the pebble now spread throughout my body. I felt soft and more forgiving toward myself.

"It is what it is," I said to Jeanne.

She agreed and suggested that I carry that mantra with me during my visit. "She is what she is," she said. "You are what you are. Sometimes that's good enough."

A few days later, I was in Allentown with my parents ready to have the difficult conversation.

"You're not getting divorced already, are you?" asked Mom. By then I had been married for two years. She and Dad sat side by side on the sofa in their living room, hands folded in their laps, looking like children who had been called into the principal's office.

"No, Rich and I are good. But we need to talk about how much longer the two of you can manage this house. Going up and down the stairs . . ."

Dad cut me off. "We manage just fine. I have a system."

I'd witnessed his system, sitting on his butt and scooting down one step at a time or crawling up them hand over hand. He was a proud man.

My mother had gone uncharacteristically quiet, studying a large liver spot on the back of her hand.

"She doesn't go into the basement anymore. I take care of the laundry when I'm doing paperwork at my desk."

"How do you get the clothes up and down the stairs?" I asked. I imagined the dirty clothes being tossed down the basement stairs.

"I told you. I have a system." My father was an engineer by profession. He had always been handy around the house. I decided not to challenge him.

"That's good, for now. But what if one of you falls and breaks a hip? Or becomes incapacitated? Wouldn't you be safer living on one floor, or in an independent living community?"

Mom sprang to life. "Your father and I are in better shape than most of our friends. We're not ready for an old folks' home."

I hadn't come to fight. Dad was eighty-one and Mom eighty-four, and they were doing well for their ages. I didn't expect them to say, "Great idea!" But my sisters and I hoped they might at least start talking more realistically about their future.

"OK. Your decision. But would you consider doing some decluttering? It's a big job, and I could help you while I'm visiting."

Actually, it was bigger than big. They were Depression-era survivors. Every closet in the four-bedroom house was stuffed with clothing and shoes they no longer wore and sheets, towels, and blankets that didn't fit in the linen closet. The drawers in the guest bedroom dressers overflowed with wrapping paper, ribbons, costume jewelry, purses. It was junk to me, treasures to them.

The basement was its own purgatory. At the bottom of the steep narrow steps was one large room. At the far end were my father's desk and file cabinets. Piles of papers covered every inch of the desk. To the left of my father's "office" were the laundry room and pantry, stockpiled with canned goods, cleaning supplies, and paper products—enough to fill the local minimart. In the other end of the basement was my mother's sewing machine and storage bins, well organized but covered in dust. It'd been years since her arthritic hands could sew on a button, let alone create an outfit. At the end of the room was a jam-packed walk-in closet.

Dad was avoiding eye contact.

"Your dad never lets me throw out anything. Especially our Tupperware containers. Can we start there?" my mother asked.

I jumped at the opening. "Yes! We can start with the kitchen cabinets, see what you have, and what you might not need anymore."

"I'll leave this to you girls," said Dad. He stood up and shuffled off to the den with the morning newspaper.

Mom and I moved to the kitchen. I opened all the cabinets so that I could get a better sense of what we were dealing with. Mom stared at the cabinet under the counter with the storage containers.

"What a mess! See what I mean? He won't throw anything away." She sat in a kitchen chair while I got on all fours and started pulling out the contents. It was a clown car. How had they fit all these lids and containers into such a small space?

"How about we start by pairing up the containers with their lids? And sorting them according to size."

"I like to keep all the lids together," said Mom.

"OK. But first let's see if you have bottoms for all these tops." I was working to stay calm. We'd had epic power struggles for years. I didn't want to get into another one over plastic lids.

"Give me those lids," said Mom. "I know which ones have bottoms."

I got busy stacking the various containers. They covered the kitchen floor. And much to my surprise they all had matching lids.

"Which ones would you like to get rid of, Mom?"

"There aren't as many as I thought. Maybe Dad's right. We just need to organize them better."

Breathe.

"Mom, you can't possibly use all these containers."

"How would you know? You don't live here anymore." There was an edge to her voice. She was sporting for a fight.

Let it go, let it go.

"True enough. I'll reorganize them so that you can see what you've got. Think about which cabinet you want to tackle next."

Mom nattered mindlessly. I tuned her out and practiced staying on point.

Soon the cabinet looked good—not so cluttered. I was pleased with myself.

You've got this, Rosanne.

Mom pointed to the cabinet above the refrigerator. "How about that one?"

It was beyond reach without a stepladder. I guessed it hadn't been opened in years. I pulled out the stepladder and climbed up. On top of the refrigerator, blocking the cabinet doors, sat a large wooden salad bowl. Underneath the bowl was a pile of placemats and cloth napkins. The bowl was filled with papers: grocery receipts, recipes clipped out of the newspaper, photos of children that used to be on the refrigerator door until they had been displaced by more recent photos.

I handed the bowl down to Mom.

"Oh, your father. He saves everything!"

I knew this pattern all too well. It was never her fault.

Breathe.

I pulled out cheap glass vases, serving bowls, knick-knacks. An utter hodgepodge.

"Mom, there's a lot of stuff up here that looks like it hasn't been touched in years. What about these vases?"

"I still use them."

"When?" I asked skeptically.

"Oh, I don't know. When somebody sends us flowers."

"Those usually come in vases, which is how you've accumulated all of these. How about we get rid of them?"

"No! I told you. I still use them."

Resistance is futile.

"OK. Well, let's take them out of this cabinet and store them in the den closet so that you can get to them when you need them." I couldn't imagine finding room in the den closet, but I was trying to create a bridge between the vases and the dump. She agreed.

We moved on to the serving bowls. "Do you still use these?" I held up one at a time, and she nodded yes emphatically each time.

With the vases gone, I arranged the bowls on one side of the cabinet. I was working up to the knick-knacks. I showed her a ceramic girl holding a basket of flowers that I'd never seen before.

"How about this, Mom? Ready to let it go?"

"No. Your Aunt Emma made that for me. I like to put it out when she visits."

Highly unlikely. She and I both knew that the ceramic girl hadn't seen the light of day in years. My patience was ebbing.

It is what it is. She is what she is.

In the back of the cabinet were two ceramic roosters that my parents used to put out every Thanksgiving.

"Oh my God, the roosters! I haven't seen these in years," I exclaimed. "How about the roosters? Ready to let go of them?"

"No, not the roosters. I love the roosters."

"But Mom, you don't use them anymore. Sooner or later you're going to need to get rid of all this stuff. Why not start with one or two things? Maybe the roosters, or the vases?" My voice had become strident.

She matched it and escalated, her eyes narrowing and her voice sharp as a razor. "You think you can come in here and tell me how to live my life? Well, Miss Smarty Pants, you have another think coming."

She glared up at me. I was precariously balanced on the stepladder, holding one of the roosters. I snapped.

"It's a stupid rooster!" I yelled, as I waved the rooster in the air. "You didn't even remember it was up here! You're just as bad as Dad! I give up."

I stepped down off the ladder and stomped out of the kitchen, headed for my old bedroom. The spiritually evolved psychotherapist and teacher in training had morphed into a screaming teenager. I felt thwarted, powerless.

I lay face down on the bed, using my pillow to muffle my sobs.

Damn. That didn't take long. Then I remembered to sense my body, to come back to my center.

A surge of spacious warmth entered my heart. I felt tender toward myself. Old patterns die hard. This one had been years in the making.

Dad, the peacemaker, knocked on the door. He, too, was locked in his own pattern of trying to smooth my and my mother's ruffled feathers.

"Rosanne, can I come in?"

"Sure, Dad."

"Your mother is very upset. She's crying in our bedroom. I think you should apologize to her."

We'd had this conversation countless times during my childhood. I'd sullenly march into their bedroom and apologize, hating her—and hating him for not taking my side. I couldn't do it that way again.

"I will, Dad. Just give me some time."

He walked out, closing the door behind him. I sat up on the bed and began to meditate. Taking deep breaths, I focused on the movement of the breath as it filled my Kath, or belly center, and then emptied out. My thoughts and emotions began to empty out too, becoming more diffuse. After twenty minutes, I stood up, grabbed the keys to my rental car, and quietly left the house.

I drove toward Lehigh Parkway. The weeping willows and creek running through the park soothed my frazzled nerves. Then I headed for the farmers' market in the Allentown fairgrounds.

The market was full of stalls selling fresh fruits and vegetables, barrels of pickles, meats, and pastries from the Amish farms on the outskirts of town. Rows and rows of delicacies that I grew up with. I was tempted to buy one of everything, but I was on a mission.

I found the stand selling perogies, dough stuffed with mashed potatoes and sharp cheddar cheese. Mom loved them, especially when they were sautéed with caramelized onions in butter and olive oil and served with a dollop of sour cream on top.

I bought a dozen and headed home.

Mom was in her favorite spot in the den, at the corner of the sofa under the floor lamp. Her eyesight was poor. She was holding a *Ladies' Home Journal* magazine up to the light so that she could read the stories.

Standing in front of her, I held out the plastic bag filled with the perogies.

"Sorry, Mom. I brought you a peace offering."

She looked up, a scowl on her face. Then she spotted the perogies. Her eyes lit up.

I smiled. "I'm going to cook some up for us now."

I walked into the kitchen, put everything back into the cabinets, and got to work sautéing the onions.

CHAPTER TWENTY

Practicing Forgiveness

Over the next few years, my mother and I gradually inched our way toward more complete forgiveness. Three years after the rooster debacle, I visited my parents in Allentown. Mom and Dad had finally agreed to sell their home and move in with my younger sister and her husband. The four of them bought a house together with an in-law unit for my parents. The house was still under construction, but my parents had drawings of the addition spread across their dining room table.

When it was time for me to return to California, I joined Mom in the den, she in her usual corner on the couch and I next to her. We were holding hands and saying our goodbyes.

"You seem at peace with the move, Mom."

"Well, it's not really what I want, but your dad can't do the stairs anymore. I hate losing my independence. I hope they don't think they can walk into our apartment anytime they want."

I gave her hand a gentle squeeze.

"By the way, Mom. Remember the training I've been in for the last seven years to become a teacher? I got ordained a few months ago."

"What does that mean, you got ordained?" she asked, as she let go of my hand and turned to look at me.

"It means I'm an ordained minister and can now teach the Diamond Approach."

She looked at me with a puzzled expression. "I still have no idea what the Diamond Approach is. My friends keep asking what you're doing these days, and I don't know what to tell them."

I laughed. It wasn't easy for me either. I often stumbled when explaining that it was a path of self-realization, a way to discover the deepest truth of our spiritual nature and the nature of all reality.

"You could tell your friends that I'm a spiritual teacher."

"Is it like being a nun?"

I paused and thought before answering. "No. It's more like being a priest."

She looked intently at me, then nodded and said, "I like that." And picked up a *People* magazine.

We sat together quietly while she read for a minute or two. Then she looked at me over the top of her magazine. "Did you know that Hugh Grant got arrested for soliciting a prostitute? Honestly, these actors make too much money for their own good."

"Yup, I heard about that." Mom loved reading about stars and their private lives. "Anything else interesting?"

She looked at her watch and tossed aside the magazine. "I didn't realize how late it was. I better get on with my novena. I've got so many people to pray for that if I don't start now, I won't be done in time to make dinner."

For as long as I could remember, Mom prayed a novena every day. She kept her prayer book and crystal rosary beads next to her magazines and newspapers on a small table by the sofa.

"Who do you pray for, Mom?"

She seemed impatient to get on with it but paused to answer. "Oh, you know. Dad, you girls, my grandkids. And my friends." She rattled off several names, none of whom I recognized.

"What do you pray for when you pray for the family?"

"I pray that your father stays healthy, and that Carolyn slows down. She works too hard. I pray that Janice stops worrying. She makes mountains out of molehills. I pray that Gregg [he added an extra g to his name when he turned eighteen] stays out of trouble, that Michael does well at Bucknell, and that Emily finds a nice husband when she grows up."

"And what about me, Mom? What do you pray for, for me?"

She shot me a look, picked up her rosary beads, and then hesitated before opening her novena book. She seemed reluctant to answer. "I pray that you'll forgive me for stopping you from becoming a nun."

"You remember that?" I asked softly. I sat in stunned silence. We'd never had a conversation about that slap in fifth grade, and it didn't look like we ever would. She had already closed her eyes and begun praying. Her mouth moved silently with each Hail Mary, working her clear crystal beads.

I slipped the black crystal mala off my wrist and began my own prayers.

PART III
Into the World

Friend, please tell me what I can do about this world
I hold to, and keep spinning out of control?
In my heart I can hear the wind passing over
the edge of the cliff.
Flowers blossom, even in the cracks of the stone.
Awake, my friend! Awake!
The beloved is calling you to join the eternal dance.

—Adapted from the poetry of Kabir,
the 15th-century Indian mystic poet

CHAPTER TWENTY-ONE

Empty, Empty

Sometimes I had fantasies of dying at the abbey or living there permanently, giving up my life in the world. A life of contemplation had appealed to me off and on for years. I had chosen the life of a householder, a spiritual practitioner who lives in the world but is not of the world, and it seemed to suit me well. And yet, I wondered some days if I had made the right choice.

When I found myself getting swept away by fantasies, I gently returned my attention to the present moment, whether that meant keeping my space clean, making daily trips to the abbey's cold storage, cooking, brewing tea in my red teapot, taking long walks, meditating, or sleeping. "All One Taste," I reminded myself. Bliss, emptiness, agitation, frustration, hunger, laziness, anger, fear—every drop of experience the same great taste of the Ocean of Being.

The morning of my sixtieth birthday, December 19, I pulled on my red heavyweight turtleneck, the only clean top left before doing my laundry. Despite my ambivalence toward the color, red became the symbolic color of this retreat: red teacup, red Durga shawl, red heart-shaped stone, the red rocks just outside my window, and the red-tailed hawk I'd see often on my walks. And just last week, I found a tiny red prayer flag in my front yard, which I added to my altar. The next day I found a green one and folded it up as a gift to Mike.

After a cup of tea, I opened a card that Mike had given me, along with my journal, as I passed through Logan Airport on my way to Halifax three weeks earlier. It seemed like a year since I had hugged him goodbye before boarding the plane. I was deeply touched by the card and that Mike had thought to tuck it into my bag so that I would have something to open on my birthday. I placed it next to the red teacup and took a photo to mark the day, sixty years on this planet. I ate my dinner of rice and broccoli slowly, savoring each bite and feeling grateful for the precious opportunity of this solitary retreat. I felt grateful, too, for my husband, my life partner, who gracefully supported my decision to take this time away to follow my inner flame.

The afternoon of Christmas Eve, I walked over to the abbey, hoping to find something festive to cook up for dinner, as I was growing weary of my diet. When I entered the kitchen, my mouth began to water at the thought of miso soup or a cheesy vegetable casserole. But the refrigerator was bare. Most of the nuns and monks had left to visit their families. I went downstairs to the cold storage, and filled my basket with a sweet potato, broccoli, carrots, and an onion.

As I walked back to my cabin, images flooded my mind of Rich visiting with his parents and sister in Mexico for the holiday. As I navigated the tundra-like conditions of the path, bundled up in layers to protect against the wind, it occurred to me that Rich was probably heading to the beach in flip flops, T-shirt, and shorts. Maybe the four of them were already lounging in comfortable chairs, slathered in sunscreen as they gazed at the Sea of Cortez. Nothing to contemplate but their next luscious meal. Were they thinking about me, missing me?

And what about my family? I imagined my sisters, their husbands and children, and my parents gathered at Janice and Dave's house in Pennsylvania, opening presents that evening around the Christmas tree. All of them laughing, talking at once: the utter chaos that is my family. Did *they* remember me? Maybe a fleeting thought from Carolyn. *I wonder how Rosanne is doing on her retreat.*

Melancholy interspersed with bliss and contentment permeated my consciousness throughout the day. By early evening, I felt flat, maybe even depressed. I reached for Dipa Ma's book, taking some comfort in her teaching that whether you were in a monastery or with your family, any way will lead to enlightenment as long as you practice mindfulness. I felt my love for my family as well as my desire to stay close to myself. For years, the two felt in conflict, and as the knot began to unwind, the tears flowed. Could I stay true to myself once I returned home?

When it was time for dinner, I went through the motions of chopping and cooking and eating but was distracted. Afterward, I sat on a cushion in front of my altar, thinking meditation would help. Instead, it created even more agitation. My altar, strewn with photos of my teachers and various Buddhas, something I had carefully created at the start of my retreat, now struck me as a cluttered mess of stuff.

In an instant, I emptied the altar of every photo and sacred stone and put them in a pile. Next, I gathered all the spiritual books I had been reading along with the one clock in the cabin and added them to the pile. *Done with you!* I gathered the heap and threw everything into my tiny bedroom closet, forcing the door shut. I didn't care where things landed. I just wanted them gone from my sight.

Afterward I sat in the unadorned space of my meditation room and let the starkness sink in. I felt both relief and sorrow. Had I realized anything about my True Nature, anything real and true about myself during these past three weeks? What did *I* know to be true versus what others taught as truth? I felt stripped bare, much like my altar. My first thought was *I could use a big bowl of vanilla ice cream*. But escape was not an option. Instead, I inquired into my sorrow and doubts, a familiar practice after years as a Diamond Approach student. I sat still for several minutes, breathing into my heart and sensing my belly, staying open and curious.

Jerry said that I would get to know my mind at this retreat and that I had! I saw my selfishness, my fears, my aversions, my attachments. I watched my sense of self dissolve and reconstitute, a dance of emptiness created by my mind. I grew more tolerant of the emptiness. And in that emptiness, there was only awareness and clarity, freed from the weight of concepts.

Gradually, my emotions shifted, replaced by a soft warmth in my chest, which then dissolved into spacious emptiness. In a spiral of timelessness, I saw my death. I had to remind myself to keep taking deep breaths as self-images peeled away like layers of an onion. Mother, daughter, wife, friend—each identity turning to dust and disappearing into the vast emptiness. Identity as teacher, as woman, felt more essential, but those, too, turned to dust. Body. Wasn't I my body? That, too, morphed into a hologram of light and energy before dispersing into space.

Emptiness gobbled up the last vestiges of the incarnation of Rosanne Sylvia Tauber Lawson Andersen Annoni. And yet something remained: pure unencumbered awareness. In that moment I finally understood, experientially, not conceptually, what the great spiritual masters teach. Most of what we take to be ourselves and take others to be are simply empty elaborated mental constructs.

I saw my loved ones, my husband Rich, my friend Mike, my son, Gregg, my family, left behind and mourning my death, wanting to hold on and eventually surrendering to the inevitable. I was gone, and all that remained was an empty hole, my earthly existence disappearing into a black abyss. The realization took my breath away. I skipped my cup of evening tea and went straight to bed.

CHAPTER TWENTY-TWO

Leaving Gampo Abbey

The vision of my death left me with the impression that my life could be forgotten quickly. Grief and loss were still concepts. I had not yet buried my mother, who would die at the age of ninety-five, a few years after this retreat. Nor had I ushered my father across the thin veil between this world and the next. He died six years after my mother at the age of ninety-six. Both deaths would be expected yet a surprise. Are we ever fully prepared for death when it happens? Even if the self is a concept and the body is temporary, and something fundamental never dies, the loss is real. I would mourn them and miss them but had yet to experience the true depths of grief.

When I awoke Christmas morning and walked into the kitchen, there was the red teacup waiting to be filled and emptied and washed and filled and emptied again. I stared at it, and although still beautiful, its nature was more apparent to me—dust destined to return to dust just like everything else in the cabin, myself included. In the immediacy of the moment, I understood the truth of impermanence. I paused to look at the photo of a raven that hung in my bedroom with a quote: *Good and bad, happy and sad, all thoughts vanish into emptiness like the imprint of a bird in the sky.*

I was surprised to feel a huge wave of relief. Even though my life was unique and valuable, it was also transient. I was not indispensable. I did not have to say yes to every person who asked something of me. I did not have to put my own needs aside for others. I did not have to work so hard to prove that I was special, to be seen and valued, to be loved.

With this realization came a profound sense of liberation from the many constraints I had imposed on myself. What remains after the emptying out of self is the certainty that what is most essential, in me and in every living being, is our indestructible True Nature. We don't have to seek love or value or meaning. We *are* love, we *are* value. All life is meaningful simply because we exist.

It was Christmas, and it was simply another day of my retreat. I drank my tea, sat in meditation, walked the path leading up to the stupa, and turned left, walking as far as the yellow house. Snow was falling heavily, erasing each step along the way. Everything the same and nothing the same. After a tumultuous day, something had settled in my consciousness, and I was content to be where I was, how I was, whether enlightened or confused. All One Taste.

It reminded me of how conflicted I felt after returning from my first Mahamudra retreat with Dan at Big Sur and how my mind eventually settled down. I continued to practice the nine steps of concentration that Dan taught, called the Elephant Path, while teaching and practicing the Diamond Approach. The two paths enhanced each other, but I worried that I needed to make a choice between them.

Some days I considered giving up the Diamond Approach with its main practice of inquiry, believing that my true path was Buddhism, its main path being meditation. What added to the confusion was that my heart felt more fully engaged in the Tibetan practices. When I sat, I imagined Dilgo Khyentse Rinpoche sitting next to me, whispering guidance on how to deepen my practice. I fell in love with Milarepa, an eleventh-century yogi who practiced in caves and lived on nettles. I joyfully sang his songs of realization at meditation classes taught by Lama Palden in San Rafael.

But then I would attend a Diamond Approach weekend or prepare a teaching for my Boston group and feel my deep connection to the path. In fact, the practice of inquiry and Hameed's precise teachings on the various aspects and dimensions of Reality had been an important factor in giving me access to Dan's teachings.

At some point along the way, it became clear that each path had its gifts and that the combination of meditation and inquiry was a potent one. Abiding in one-pointed stillness is essential for perceiving reality without the distortions of our ordinary mind. Inquiry is a tool that enables us to work with those distortions and other barriers to clear awareness, and to discover the mysteries of Reality. How wonderful and fortunate I was to have found both.

I was also heartened to notice that the path of Catholicism still lived in my soul. Sometimes I turned to prayer when I was having difficulty calming my mind or staying with the pain of my history, remembering the words of the prayer of my beloved ecstatic, St. Teresa of Avila.

Let nothing disturb you.

Anytime I forgot my nature—True Nature or God—I prayed for assistance to abide in the truth. When I was present again in the totality of my nature, I was awash in gratitude. In time, I noticed that the imaginary distinctions I made in my mind between Catholicism, Buddhism, and the Diamond Approach dissolved. All true paths bring us directly into contact with our deepest nature even if how they are articulated is different.

Only One. One Taste. All the same sweet taste of the Divine.

If an ancient crone had told me how long to stay at Gampo Abbey, it might have sounded something like, "When the moving waters stand still, it will be time to leave." The river below my cabin had frozen over in the past week. Outer and inner waters were still. It was time.

On the morning of my departure, I carefully tucked some chai tea leaves into the red teacup, wrapped it in tissue paper, secured it with a mala, and placed it in my shoulder bag.

Jerry offered to drive me back to the café, a precious opportunity for one last visit. Ours had developed into a collegial relationship, me sharing perspectives of the Diamond Approach and him opening my mind and heart to the teachings of Trungpa.

During the drive back, I was aware of feeling more present, softer, and more expansive than when I had arrived. The stark landscape of Cape Breton in winter had grown on me, and I was sorry to leave so soon. But I was looking forward to returning to my life and reuniting with my husband, friends, and family. As we traveled along the narrow highway, I savored each moment. Jerry parked the car in front of the café and helped me unload my suitcases. As a thank you, I offered him the red teacup.

"Remember to add honey!"

"May you go easy," Jerry said as he accepted my gift.

"You as well."

The flight home was effortless, the benefit of a month of practice. I had a layover in Boston, and there was Mike, ever faithful, waiting for me as I walked off the plane, in the days after 9/11 and enhanced security. It was 6:00 p.m. on New Year's Eve. The airport was virtually empty, and we easily found a quiet table in a café. Mike ordered tea for us, and we sipped it slowly as we sat across from each other.

"Your eyes are windows to the universe. I can see the fruits of your retreat in them," said Mike.

"It was beyond amazing, Mike," I said. "At times difficult but mostly illuminating. And your card, thank you! It made my birthday."

Mike smiled; I smiled. We sat and looked at each other, radiating our ageless love and mutual appreciation. We held hands across the table, and when it was time for me to board, we acknowledged the time with a squeeze of the hands.

As I boarded the plane to San Francisco, my heart was brimming with love and gratitude. I settled into my seat, unaware of the passage of time, and was surprised when the plane touched down just before midnight. Rich was waiting for me at my gate, looking like an apparition of kindness and love.

"Happy New Year," he said, as he enfolded me in his arms.

Now the journey of living in the world but not of it would begin in earnest.

CHAPTER TWENTY-THREE

Back to Reality

For the first few weeks after my return from the abbey, resuming my ordinary life was effortless. Teaching, relating to my husband and family was different from the solitary life in my cabin, but my inner state remained stable. When my familiar sense of self arose, it was eclipsed by a truer self, grounded in the perspective of Oneness. From that perspective, it made no sense to be self-centered, reactive, or defensive.

And yet my external life could not have been further from the simplicity of my inner nature. I had a full practice of private students each week, two Diamond Approach inquiry groups, each meeting once a month, and three Diamond Approach teaching groups. The groups met once every four to six weeks on weekends, so I spent much of my time between private sessions preparing the teachings and answering emails related to administration of the groups. On average I taught two weekends a month. As much as I enjoyed all aspects of teaching, I wondered if I'd taken on too much.

In addition to traveling to Boston every few months to teach the group there, I traveled to the United Kingdom twice a year to assist two large retreat groups taught by Sandra Maitri, a highly regarded teacher of both the Diamond Approach and the Enneagram. Although the travel and long hours at the retreats took their toll on my physical body, I loved being in Wales and learning from Sandra's teachings. Afterward we would reward ourselves with a trip to London, shopping at Harrods or visiting museums.

Over the years, Sandra and I became close friends, which added to the enjoyment of work in the UK. Twice a year, I combined my time in the UK with a trip to Bremen, Germany, to assist at a group there as well. The downside was that, between traveling and working at retreat groups, the entire trip meant three weeks away from home.

I returned to a backlog of emails and phone messages, and a husband who had been left with caring for our two aging cats, paying bills, grocery shopping, and cooking, all while maintaining his own private practice as a psychologist. He often felt, rightfully so, that my teaching schedule dominated our lives. It took precedence over everything, including when we could take vacations or spend time together on weekends.

We were both prisoners of my ambitious work schedule. Because teaching served to deepen my realization, for many years I confused spiritual practice with teaching and felt justified in making it my priority. The insight I'd had at Gampo Abbey, about not needing to say yes to everything just because it was beneficial, proved challenging to put into practice.

In May 2007, after a teaching trip to the UK, I met my husband at the Frankfurt airport on our way to a dream vacation in Greece. He had arranged most of the details, and we were both looking forward to time alone, away from the stresses of work and daily living. We travel well together, and neither of us had been to Greece. For two luxurious weeks we visited ruins in Athens, shopped in Mykonos, wandered the beaches and countryside of Crete, and watched magenta and orange sunsets from our room in Santorini. We walked, made love, and gorged on Greek salads, unusual lamb dishes, and yogurt smothered in honey.

The trip was rejuvenating for our relationship and for me. With no work to pull me away, I was able to relax and enjoy time with my husband and time with myself. I read novels for pleasure rather than transcripts for teaching or spiritual books for enlightenment. We meditated most mornings but in a relaxed manner. Though I was not focused on spiritual practice, I remained present to my inner nature. It gave me a taste of what my life could feel like if I had more space to *just be* the way I had at Gampo Abbey.

That potential space filled up quickly. Within a month of our return from Greece, Rich's mother was diagnosed with a brain tumor. Tests and surgery revealed metastasized cancer, and for the next ten months, our lives were turned upside down. Rich's parents lived in Southern California, and his father was showing signs of dementia. Once his mother returned home from the hospital, it fell on Rich and his sister to take care of their parents. Mame lived in Seattle and spent weeks at a time in Long Beach, with Rich coming as often as his schedule allowed. I would join them when I could, shopping and cooking large quantities of food they could pull from the freezer in my absence. When it became clear that Joyce was terminal, we took on the huge task of sorting through their house and two-car garage filled with fifty-two years of accumulated possessions.

Joyce, who made few demands, had one request: that we spend Christmas on Maui. She and Ed had taken the family there for years, for either Thanksgiving or Christmas. She wanted to see the white sand beaches and dip her feet in the warm ocean water, surrounded by family, once more before she died. We scrambled to find an opening on Kaanapali Beach, her favorite. The entire family, including my son, Gregg, and the woman he was dating, put everything aside to make it happen.

Days were spent poolside, in a rented cabana facing the ocean, so that Joyce could lie comfortably watching the comings and goings of families splashing in the pool or surfing the waves. She needed a walker to get around, and we took turns sitting with her in the shade of our cabana.

"I sure would like to put my feet in the water," Joyce said on our third day there. Gregg, his girlfriend, Rich, and Mame jumped to attention. The walker wasn't an option on sand, so two of them stood on either side of her, holding her up and guiding her down to the edge of the water. Ed, her husband, watched helplessly off to the side. I followed with my camera and captured the moment, knowing it was the last time Joyce would feel the Pacific Ocean on her skin.

The next day, Gregg's girlfriend, Mame, and I went into Lahaina to do some Christmas shopping. It had been our tradition over the years to browse the shops together with Rich, Ed, and Joyce, pointing to things we wanted for Christmas. I christened it *woo woo* shopping because if one of us pointed while saying *woo woo*, that would be the signal for someone else in the group to make sure it ended up in a stocking or under a decorated palm tree. We went through the motions with heavy hearts, managing to fill stockings that we passed around on Christmas Eve.

When we returned from Hawai'i, we hired a full-time live-in caretaker to stay with Joyce and Ed even though someone from the family was usually present as well. In March, Joyce passed away with Rich at her side. We moved his dad to an assisted care facility near us in San Rafael and arranged to sell the house that Rich's parents had lived in since he was a youngster.

If it hadn't been clear to me before, this family crisis highlighted how inflexible my schedule was. No time for relaxation, for time alone to practice, for time with my husband. It wasn't a new insight, but now I was seeing the deeper truth: there was no time for life to happen, for the unexpected miracles and tragedies that are the stuff of living. If I wanted to be present for my life, to practice being in the world but not of it, I needed to learn how to say no. I compiled a list of everything I was doing as a Diamond Approach teacher and began the serious work of finding balance.

CHAPTER TWENTY-FOUR

My Mother Leaves This World

It was clear that, between trips to Long Beach and working full-time, Rich and I were stretched to our limits. Though I had compiled a list of ways to cut back, it was hard to let go. I loved teaching, loved my students, loved spending time with my husband, family, and friends. I wanted it all and had difficulty accepting my limitations. It was then I realized that integrating the experiences of my time at Gampo Abbey was going to take years, not weeks or months.

When my younger sister, Janice, phoned in January 2008, asking me to come home as soon as possible, I feared I might go over the edge. My parents were by then living with Janice and her husband, and my ninety-four-year-old mother had just been rushed to the hospital by ambulance. It wasn't clear if she'd had a stroke, but she was comatose when the paramedics arrived. I canceled my appointments for the rest of the week and took a red-eye to Allentown.

I arrived at the hospital the next morning to find my mother sitting up in her bed, fully alert and about to get a pacemaker.

My father was protesting vehemently, waving a *Do Not Resuscitate* document in her doctor's face. The doctor was patiently explaining that inserting a pacemaker was mandatory, not lifesaving, once it had been established that my mother was otherwise in good health.

"Good health" is relative. My mother was crippled by arthritis, hard of hearing, blind in one eye, and could barely get around with her walker before her collapse. My father, who hobbled around with a cane but really needed his own walker, spent most of his time tending to my mother: counting out her pills, preparing meals, fetching the heating pad or ice pack to soothe her pain, and listening to her incessant complaints.

When my mother could no longer navigate a walker and was confined to a wheelchair, the decision was made to transfer her to a nursing home. The hope was that, with some rehabilitation, she might regain enough mobility to return home. After two months of physical therapy, it was clear that she would remain in the nursing home for the rest of her life.

My mother hated losing her independence and being separated from her husband. She harassed him with calls day and night, insisting that she could walk and that he take her home.

On one of my visits to her in the nursing home, she complained bitterly.

"I get around," she said. "They aren't helping me in physical therapy. They have me folding napkins. Can you believe it? All the money it costs to be here, and I'm doing their laundry."

"I think it's a way to build up strength in your hands," I reasoned even though reasoning with my mom was like spitting in the wind.

"Ha, it's a way to get cheap labor! And you should see the meals they feed me. If your dad wasn't so tight with money, I'd be able to eat what the other people eat."

Mom had difficulty picking up food with utensils, so she was being served finger food. She wasn't suffering from dementia in the classic sense: She knew where she was, read the papers daily, was oriented to time and place, and recognized every member of her family. But her psychological issues, which we had all learned to live with, created problems for her on her unit. Eventually she was transferred to a dementia unit where staff was more familiar with how to deal with "difficult" patients.

The day Mom was moved, Rich and I flew to Allentown to give Janice and Dave some relief and to help ease my mother in her transition. The staff was kind and skillful. Their one requirement was that residents eat together in the small dining room. My mother was vehemently refusing to go. The head nurse encouraged us not to engage in any attempts to have a logical conversation with Mom and instead "guide her gently" toward what was expected of her.

They obviously didn't know my mother could never be guided, gently or otherwise, to do anything she didn't want to do. Still, I tried as Rich watched silently.

"We're going back to the house for a rest. The nurse will be here soon to take you to lunch."

"Talk to her. Tell her I want to eat here."

We went through a few iterations of me evading her demands and assuring her we'd be back soon. My mother became more insistent. As I turned to leave, she flew into a rage. Grabbing the orange, brown, and white crocheted blanket covering her legs, she threw it at my face, screeching, "You're chicken! That's what you are, a chicken. You're afraid of them, aren't you? Chicken, chicken!"

Rich and I turned and walked out of the room, our eyes downcast as other residents stared. We left her flailing in her wheelchair. He'd heard plenty of stories about her temper tantrums but had never seen one up close and personal.

"Is she going to be OK?" he asked, clearly shaken.

"She'll be fine by the time we return."

And she was.

In early April 2009 my sister phoned to let me know that my mother had been rushed to the hospital with a serious urinary tract infection. She was hallucinating, speaking Italian, and it wasn't clear if she would live through the night. I caught the red-eye to Allentown and arrived at the hospital the next morning. By then the antibiotics had kicked in, and my mother's delirium had subsided. But she was weak, and her prognosis not good. The parish priest was called to administer the late rites, which by then had a new name: the sacrament of "Anointing the Sick."

I was alone with my mother when Monsignor Murphy arrived, waving briskly to me as he rushed to my mother's side.

"Sylvia, my dear, how are you feeling?" he asked as he enveloped both of her hands in his. My mother sat bolt upright and startled us both by planting a kiss on his lips.

"Oh, Monsignor, thank you for coming," she said, reaching for his hands when he took a step back. From his jacket pocket, he unfurled a small black pouch with vials of oil. Within moments, he had made the sign of the cross on my mother's forehead, heart, and both hands, mumbling prayers in Latin.

And then he was gone. He flew in and out of the room before I realized that he had administered the sacrament. If I'd known, I would have joined him in prayer or at the very least stood by his side in silent meditation.

Despite our conflicts over the years, I had made peace with my mother. I remained by her bedside for another hour, holding her hand while she slept and wordlessly thanked her for all she had sacrificed over the years. I couldn't appreciate her as a child, often feeling beaten down by her unpredictable mean streak. But as I aged and matured, I had come to value the complexity of her nature. She was devoted to her husband and children. We were her life, and she pawed at us the way she pawed at Monsignor. We recoiled, like him, but remained completely loyal.

Three days after her admission to the hospital, my mother was placed on hospice and transferred back to the nursing home. Once she was stable, I returned to California to take care of some teaching responsibilities and to pack more substantially for a longer stay in Allentown. When I returned a week later, my mother had transformed into a love bunny. Gone was the tiger, poised for a fight. The arthritic pain that had crippled and tangled her body into knots was numbed by a slow drip of morphine, her rattled nerves soothed with increased doses of Ativan.

As soon as she saw me, she stretched out her arms, beckoning me to come closer. I embraced her, falling into her bed to get as close as I could. She strained to reach my face with her lips, kissing me repeatedly and saying, "I love you. I love you."

When I stepped back from her embrace, my mother was aglow, a soft smile on her face. Within moments, a nurse entered to take her temperature, and I watched the scene repeat, but this time with the nurse. "I love you. I love you," her arms stretched out to embrace the nurse.

And so it was, with each person who entered the room. My irascible mother was now freely planting kisses on lips and expressing love to whoever attended to her. Rather than feeling diminished by this indiscriminate show of affection, I celebrated. Free now of the barriers of emotional and physical pain, my mother was returning to the Light and Love of her True Nature, the potential that lives in each of us human beings.

Throughout the death vigil, I remained in a state of consciousness reminiscent of my many meditation retreats and my time at Gampo Abbey. My heart was an open field of compassion, nothing excluded. As I observed my father sitting on the edge of his walker, bent over the side of my mother's bed to hold her hand, I felt only love and appreciation for him too.

My mother's funeral took place, poignantly, the day after Mother's Day in May 2009. By this time my son, Gregg, had graduated from the University of San Francisco and was living in the city. A month to the day after Gregg's graduation from college in 2004, his father died of a heart attack. He was sixty-three years old and had lived life on his own terms, unwilling to give up the bacon and eggs, steaks, and cigarettes that he loved despite two triple bypass surgeries. It was a devastating blow to Gregg, who adored his father. A few weeks after Al's death, Gregg got into a motorcycle accident and tore up his knee. He was grieving, without a job, and now without mobility. Rich and I offered him financial support to pay for an apartment until he could function on his own.

This was not the first time we supported Gregg financially, and it had never been easy. Gregg liked doing what he wanted to do and bristled at any hint of interference from us. He was a sullen fifteen years old when Rich and I got together, and Gregg barely tolerated his presence. By his senior year of high school, Gregg was skipping classes, and his grades were too low to apply to college. He begged his father and us to send him to prep school, at a hefty cost. Within five months, Gregg was kicked out of the prep school for getting inebriated along with another classmate.

This was the start of the deterioration of my relationship with Gregg. Rich and I were pretty sure he had a substance abuse problem, which Gregg vehemently denied. He would disappear for days or weeks, not return my phone calls or texts. And then he'd show up as if nothing were amiss. I started to think of him as "the little girl who had a little curl right in the middle of her forehead." When he was good, he was very, very good: loving, jovial, affectionate. And when he was bad, he was horrid: sullen, critical, withholding. My heart ached for the beautiful human being I knew him to be. The ten-year-old boy who said, "Told you she was pretty," when I picked him and his friend up from school one day. The boy who would massage my shoulders when I'd had a long day.

"I wish you'd known him when he was little," I'd say to Rich. I'd read enough books to know I had a codependent relationship with Gregg, fueled by my guilt and insecurities. But I was too scared to set firm boundaries, like "get help with your substance abuse if you want us to support you." I didn't want to risk losing him, which created tension between me and Rich, who was a psychologist working with addictions. We were both held hostage by Gregg, me wanting a relationship with Gregg and Rich not wanting to lose me. He had to bite his tongue when what he really wanted to do was confront Gregg.

At some point, Gregg became a successful mortgage broker, making his own money and spending it as fast as he made it. We tried to encourage him to start saving, which only infuriated Gregg.

"I want to enjoy my life, not sacrifice for the future the way you and Rich do. I like living on the high wire," he said one time when I met him for lunch in San Francisco.

"I know you do, and it scares the hell out of me. What if you lose your job or get sick and can't work," I asked.

"Oh, Mom, you're old school. I'll be fine."

When he lost his money and condo in the financial crash of 2008, my worst fears came true. He scrambled to find a job, to keep his relationship intact with his girlfriend, and once again turned to us for financial support. This time around was even more painful than when he was younger. He had been on his own and didn't want to answer to me or Rich. His mantra was "I want to do whatever I want to do." Kind of like me when I married Al over my parents' objections. Except I wasn't abusing substances, and I wasn't asking them for money.

As parents, did we make some of our own bad decisions? Yes. Thinking we could fix him or change him only alienated Gregg further. By the time of my mother's funeral, Gregg was barely speaking to us. His preferred way of communicating was through long emails raging at me for not being on his side.

"I'm a Lawson, not an Annoni. I need to be around people who support me for who I am, and you don't."

I wanted to scream an email response to him, maybe all caps.

"IT'S ALL I'VE EVER WANTED FOR YOU! WHY DO YOU THINK I INSCRIBED YOUR BABY BOOK WITH THE QUOTE *IF YOU LOVE SOMEONE, SET THEM FREE; IF THEY COME BACK, THEY'RE YOURS; IF THEY DON'T, THEY NEVER WERE.*"

Instead, sometimes I tried to explain my concerns, sometimes I deleted his emails because they were so toxic. In my naivete, I had imagined my son soaring. Instead, I watched him crash and burn over and over again, me standing by helplessly, unable to save him. Waiting for years for him to come back, which he eventually did. But it was a very long wait.

Despite our differences, Gregg loved his Nana and wanted to come to the funeral. We paid his airfare and planned for him to stay with us at my sister's home. The morning of the funeral, Rich, Gregg, and I drove together to the church. I was subdued but calm until I saw the hearse parked in front of the church. In that moment, my mother's death became a reality, and I started sobbing. Rich reached over to take my hand, and Gregg leaned forward from the back seat to rub my shoulders. For the next few hours, we were a united family, the conflicts receding in our shared sorrow.

CHAPTER TWENTY-FIVE

Estrangement from My Son, Back into Therapy

The détente with Gregg was short-lived. When Gregg disowned us two months later, I sank into a deep depression the way I had in 1985 after he moved in with his dad, and Mike broke off our relationship. The years of Reichian therapy and spiritual inquiry were not touching this recurrent despondency. I didn't know where to turn for help but knew I needed to do something.

After a tearful few months, Rich encouraged me to consider therapy. I had my doubts, believing I had already gotten everything I could from a psychotherapeutic approach to problems. A dear friend, who was also a teacher in the Diamond Approach, convinced me to consider seeing the therapist she was working with. She described Barbara as extraordinary, someone with both a spiritual and psychological approach, and a long waiting list.

Barbara used a system called Bodynamics, a somatic developmental psychology that unwinds early defensive patterns of connecting and relating. My friend was finding Bodynamics a powerful adjunct to the Diamond Approach in that both use the body as a resource to return to our fundamental nature. Though I had misgivings, I made the call and got on Barbara's waiting list. A month later, in desperation, I called Barbara again and begged her to fit me in wherever she could.

Barbara had a kind but no-nonsense approach. Each time I resisted digging deeper, she encouraged me to face my worst fear, which turned out to be abandonment. We delved into my history, starting with my early separation from my mother when she hemorrhaged during childbirth.

Prior to my mother's death, I suspected there might be more to the story and had asked Mom what it was like for her when she came home from the hospital after hemorrhaging for the second time.

"I took to the couch," she said.

This was news to me. I'd always thought of my mom as a dynamo who stayed busy morning till night. I pressed for more details. Reluctantly, she admitted that she couldn't do anything for a while.

"How long is 'a while'? A few days, a few weeks, a few months?" I asked.

"Oh, about six months."

What? Was she suffering from postpartum depression, or PTSD after the traumatic delivery, or afraid that if she moved, she would bleed to death? Maybe all three. Pieces of the puzzle of my life fell into place, including my strong attachment to my Nonna. My mother and I were enmeshed, but that's not the same as being attached.

When I shared this info with Barbara, she nodded, as if she already knew.

"You're suffering from abandonment depression, which lives in your psyche like a slow-moving stream. It turns into a raging river whenever you feel abandoned by someone you love," she said. "You have what we call in the trade attachment issues. Yours was an insecure or ambivalent attachment."

Finally, a name for my ambivalence in relationships and why I had difficulty tolerating them when things got tough. Rather than risking the pain of abandonment, I left. I also began to understand why I thought I wasn't a good mother to my son. I wasn't abusive like my mother, but I think I fell short of offering him a secure attachment. Perhaps it's no wonder that he disowned me when things got difficult between us. He learned from a pro.

In my heart I longed for a son who was more like me, who valued spirituality and was open to talking about his feelings with me. A son who embraced the life I had imagined for him, which included partnership and children. I imagine that Gregg longed for parents who were more easygoing like his father. Rich and I took things too seriously for his tastes.

During an interview for the *New York Times*, Glenda Jackson, the famous British politician and actress, said, "I think you have done quite well as a parent if your kid holds positions totally opposite to your own."

Oh, to have had a mother like her, or to have been that kind of a mother to my son.

Instead, I was burdened with guilt and shame about Gregg's choices. I wonder if this was how my mother felt, when I chose to marry a Black man. I knew she was worried about what her friends would think, but what else was she feeling? Perhaps hurt that her daughter didn't seem to be interested in what mattered most to *her*. Mom's response was to disown me, much like Gregg's. My response to both of them was to blame myself for their upsets with me.

But what I believe to be our saving grace is that we human beings are more than our personality, more than our history, more than our mistakes. If we are fortunate enough to discover our essential nature, and to come to identify as *that,* rather than our personality, we can experience the joy of liberation. If not for this truth, we would all be doomed to a life of endless suffering.

CHAPTER TWENTY-SIX

Deepening Friendship

Mike was a constant in my life. I counted on him to reflect what was developing within me and to confront me about those places where I was stuck in old patterns. He knew the truth because he was an integral part of my life since my late twenties, a reliable critic and solid support.

Given the importance of our relationship, my hope was that Mike and Rich would become friends. I couldn't imagine a life without either of them in it. Eight months into my long-distance relationship with Rich, back in 1990, we arranged a rendezvous in Boston to meet Mike's boyfriend of one year, Moe, and to introduce them both to Rich. We stayed at a hotel in Back Bay near Mike's condo and had dinner together at a neighborhood restaurant. I was on edge, wanting Mike to like Rich and Rich to like Mike. Mike had stopped drinking alcohol by then, but the rest of us eased our nerves with cocktails. I liked Moe, a sweet and funny man who stayed in the background while Mike took center stage, regaling us with stories about how they met and their plans to move in together.

The next day was sunny and warm, a beautiful July summer day in the city. We walked for miles, through Boston Gardens and the Commons, down to the wharf where we indulged in creamy clam chowder and Caesar salads, then back through historic graveyards. Mike cooked dinner for us that evening, seemingly in good spirits, but I couldn't tell what he was thinking. Rich, being naturally shy, joined Moe in the background as Mike and I finished each other's sentences and talked about everything from our psychotherapy practices to the latest books we'd both read.

Later, after I returned to San Francisco and Rich to Salt Lake, I phoned Mike.

"So, what did you think of Rich?" I asked with some trepidation.

"He's very sweet and handsome to boot. But I have my concerns. Moe and I think he's gay."

That was not what I expected to hear! I said I doubted it highly, based on our sexual relationship, but Mike was not convinced.

"I just don't want you to make another bad choice, Rose," he said.

After we hung up, I raged at Mike in my head. *You never like anyone I fall in love with. Some things never change.*

There were a few more brief visits over the next six years, but I still couldn't tell if Mike and Rich were merely tolerating each other or if they were growing on each other. I wondered, too, if Moe liked me or found me a threat to his relationship with Mike. There was only one way to find out.

A year after our wedding, Rich and I traveled to the East Coast to celebrate our anniversary. After landing in Boston in early fall, we headed north to the White Mountains in New

Hampshire. Though small compared with western mountain ranges, they were still magnificent in their full autumn regalia. We stayed in a small inn in the heart of the White Mountains, hiking and exploring the area. It delighted me to watch Rich's amazement as he discovered the beauty of this very different terrain.

Next, we traveled up the coast of Maine to Bar Harbor, hiking in Acadia National Park and scoring the best lobster rolls in the world at a road stand. Our second, and last night there, we splurged on a dinner of lobsters that tasted as if they'd just been pulled from the sea.

After our time in Maine, we headed south to Cape Cod, where Mike and Moe owned a second home. I'd been to the Cape several times, but it was a first for Rich. I wanted him to love it as much as I did, and the weather cooperated. Blue skies, cool temperatures, maple leaves turning golden and maroon, bird songs filling the air.

Mike and Moe had been living together for seven years and were more at ease with each other. Rich and I were more settled together too. Mike, sensing my anxiety, put my mind at ease as soon as we arrived.

"I've been counting the days. Welcome, welcome!" he said, smiling broadly and throwing his arms around both of us. Moe was in the garden, weeding, but came in to greet us with a fistful of black-eyed Susans.

We stayed three nights with "the boys," as we came to refer to them, exploring the many kettle ponds and white sand beaches that are unique to the Cape. As food lovers, we bonded over yes, more lobsters, at the Captain Cass lobster shack in a place where Mike and I had eaten many times to celebrate the end of a Transactional Analysis treatment weekend in Rock Harbor with his clients. Captain Cass is a tiny shack overlooking Cape Cod Bay, with food served on paper plates. The four of us sat at the counter in our plastic bibs, butter dripping down our chins, in crustacean ecstasy.

Days were idyllic, sitting outdoors, watching fish jump in the pond and a plethora of birds feasting on the many feeders in Mike and Moe's backyard. Moe hung a hammock between two trees, big enough for Rich and me to read or nap in after exploring the Cape during the mornings. When it came time to say goodbye, I felt a twinge of not wanting to leave, either Mike or the Cape. As much as I loved living in California, the East Coast felt like home.

As I had hoped, Rich became enchanted with the Cape, so much so that we started visiting Mike and Moe more frequently. On one of our drives back to the airport, I had a vision of me working on the Cape. I had no idea how that would happen, since Mike and I were no longer doing treatment weekends together. I shared the vision with Rich, even though it seemed far-fetched. A few years later, after I'd been ordained as a Diamond Approach teacher, I was invited to assist at retreats in Craigsville on Cape Cod. The group met twice a year in May and October. The vision became a reality and deepened my trust in my inner guidance, a quiet voice that I was hearing more frequently, a voice that bypassed my ordinary mind.

We began a ritual of staying with Mike and Moe over the Memorial Day weekend. While I assisted at the retreat in Craigsville, Rich stayed with the boys. I joined them for two more days of vacation, the four of us indulging in ice cream at the Ice Cream Café and long walks on Hardings Beach. In time, our connection deepened into a true couples' friendship.

Octobers I traveled alone to the Cape to assist at the fall retreat and then spend a few days with Mike. Moe was still working at Children's Hospital in Boston during the week, which left Mike and me lots of free time to catch up. We liked to meet at the house after Mike's AA meeting, stop at Dunkin' Donuts for his second big cup of coffee, and then head to Hardings.

We took the same route down the sandy path that cut through beach shrub toward the lighthouse, turned left on the beach, and walked as far as we could before turning around and heading back along the water's edge. Mike was truly a creature of habit.

"I never get tired of this," he said on one of our walks.

"Me either. You're lucky to live in such a special place. Remember the first time I visited the Cape in 1977? You, Betts, Ginny, and I christened ourselves The Stroke Buddies."

"How could I forget?" Mike said. "That was at least a lifetime ago. So much has changed, meeting Mark, losing him to AIDS, getting sober and meeting Moe, you meeting Rich. We're in a good place now, Rose, aren't we?"

"We are indeed. I'm so grateful we found our way back to each other. We needed that break to get truly separate and find our mates."

We walked on for several minutes in silence, smelling the sea air and listening to the sand crunch beneath our feet.

"I still have a dream of us living down the street from each other," Mike said. "It feels possible now more than ever. We like each other's husband, no small feat. And you both like the Cape. Would you consider moving?"

His question took me aback. I'd been in California for close to thirty years and was just beginning to miss the East Coast. My parents were getting old, and I felt the tug to live closer to them.

"I do think about it, but Rich is a California guy. I'm not sure he could survive the winters here," I said. "But truth be told, I feel more at home here than I do in California."

"Oh, Rose, it would thrill me beyond the beyond if you moved back! I'm putting that out to the Universe."

"Sounds like a plan!" I said as he laughed his hearty laugh.

CHAPTER TWENTY-SEVEN

Introducing Mike to the Diamond Approach

Many of my conversations with Mike were about spirituality. We'd both been raised Catholic and, as adults, dabbled in various spiritual and metaphysical pursuits. Unlike me, Mike abhorred anything that smacked of religion. He was initially skeptical about my involvement in the Diamond Approach, concerned that I had joined a cult. The name, which sounds more metaphysical than spiritual, didn't help. To this day, I watch people's eyes glaze over when asked what I do. *A spiritual teacher where? The diamond what?* It's easier to just say, "I teach meditation."

I had my own dream that Mike would become a student of the Diamond Approach and that we could explore the teachings together. But I knew better than to push him. Like me, he did not want to feel controlled.

In 2004 the main teacher of the Boston group, Duncan, decided to start a new group. He invited me to co-teach, which meant traveling to Boston six times a year, including the two Cape retreats. Mike had noticed how the work was changing me.

"You seem more at peace with yourself, Rose. Are you?"

"I am. You more than anyone know how much I hated myself. I still do, at times, but I've learned how to be more curious about it when it happens, rather than going down that hole with my old stories," I said.

"I could use that skill. How did you learn it?"

"From endless hours of inquiry. I found it to be the missing piece in my other spiritual practices, learning now to stay with my difficult emotions long enough to understand their roots. I'd love for you to consider joining the new group in Boston. Plus, we'd get to see each other every other month! I could stay with you and Moe whenever I come to Boston to teach."

Mike was more curious than skeptical. As a recovering alcoholic, he was searching for a way to feel "high" without the use of substances. After our conversation, he decided to join the group.

We kept the depth of our friendship private, though students knew that I stayed with him and Moe while I was in town. He fondly referred to me as "Teach," both in public and in our car rides back and forth to the campus where the group met. He was a bright student, curious and dedicated and very popular among his fellow students. I got to observe him at somewhat of a distance, seeing how seductive he was with both men and women. But it was the women who swarmed around him, each vying for a special place in his heart. It reminded me of our days in Transactional Analysis training, with Ginny, Betts, and I competing for his attention.

Like me, Mike attracted people to him naturally, though back then I wasn't aware of my own charisma. My tendency was to idealize Mike, believing that he was more popular and more accomplished than me. In truth, he was more traveled, more studied in the arts, and more well-read. When I wasn't busy comparing myself with him, I relied on Mike to broaden my worldview and experiences.

Mike, too, got to observe me from afar. He had known me as a successful therapist since we worked together for years but had no idea what I was like as a teacher, having only heard about my doubts and insecurities. Prior to teaching my first weekend in Boston, he watched me fret and fuss over my talks.

After that weekend, Mike and I had a long discussion about the reality of my competence versus my inadequate self-image. Though he wasn't surprised, he was not prepared for the confident, grounded, clear teacher who showed up once I was sitting in front of the students. The next time I expressed concern about my capacity to teach, Mike confronted me.

"Why do you torture yourself with something that isn't true?"

"Old habit, I guess," I responded. But it got me thinking. If I was going to enjoy what I loved, teaching, I'd need to update my self-image.

Over the years of him being a student in the Diamond Approach, Mike would often turn to me with questions about spiritual concepts that weren't entirely clear to him.

"What do you mean by 'soul'? I only know what I learned in Catholic school. I think of it as a kidney-shaped blob with a black smudge, but I don't think that's what you're teaching."

I laughed at his image. "Nope, nothing like that. Think of it as your personal consciousness, your thoughts, feelings, sensations, historical patterns, your deepest nature. Everything that you are, nothing excluded. And no black smudge!"

Though I was the teacher and he my student, we didn't get caught in a power differential. Our long friendship set the tone for our conversations, which were illuminating for both of us. The more I explained concepts to him, the clearer they became for me. Mike grew to respect the Diamond Approach, and our spiritual connection deepened.

CHAPTER TWENTY-EIGHT

A Dream Comes True

After years of Memorial Day visits with Mike and Moe on Cape Cod, they started to tease us about buying our own house. By now, the four of us were close friends and had found a way to make space for the special relationship between Mike and me. Moe playfully called me Mike's wife, the one he could talk to about his feelings. And Rich referred to Mike as my other husband.

We spent countless hours walking around Trout Pond, picking out which houses we hoped would go on the market, even though owning two homes was out of the question financially and our lives were anchored in the Bay Area. Still, we played along. "When a house comes available on the pond," we'd say.

Soon after Rich's mother died in 2008, Moe called us to tell us about a house for sale on Pickerel Pond, across a road from Trout Pond. The timing was serendipitous. Rich and his sister had just sold the family house in Long Beach and were looking to invest in another property.

Prior to visiting Mike and Moe, Rich and I discussed the pros and cons of buying a home on the Cape and decided against it. But on our third day of walking the neighborhood, as we approached the For Sale sign, I heard a voice. *You need to look at that house.* By now, I was familiar with the voice of guidance and knew not to ignore it.

"We need to look at that house," I said to Rich.

"OK, let's call the realtor."

I was surprised at his quick and positive response. We called the realtor as soon as we got back to Mike and Moe's. Within an hour, Moe, Rich, and I were walking through the house. It felt inviting and comfortable. After getting the OK from Rich's sister, who would be one of the owners, we made an offer that was immediately accepted. By July 2008, we owned a house just four doors down the street from the boys, fulfilling Mike's dream.

The house on Pickerel Pond was like an aviary, situated on a heavily treed piece of land overlooking the pond. Because of the water and trees, it attracted the many breeds of birds that the Cape is famous for. I was besotted. We filled the house with furniture that we shipped from Long Beach and a few pieces we bought from a secondhand store in Chatham.

The house was dated but very livable. Built in the early '70s, it was a ranch style set down from the road. A wall and a pass-through opening separated the white and blue kitchen from the dining room, which faced the pond. The stove was set into a corner, making it hard for more than one person to access. The current owners had tried to open up the kitchen by putting in a counter that separated it from the living room at the front of the house. To do that, they had taken down a wall but left a pillar to support the ceiling. It felt hodgepodge to me but still had a sweet vibe that was inviting.

The recreation room off the kitchen, which sat over the pond, had cheap paneled walls, a large fireplace that had been painted black, and a tiny bar area papered with various bottles of booze. Not at all our style! The two bathrooms were classic 1970: one with a blue bathtub and toilet, blue and black tiles, the pipes rusted but working. The bathroom in the master bedroom was pink and green, a narrow space with a toilet, and a cement shower that was always cold. The bedroom itself, overlooking the pond, screamed for a remodel. We imagined replacing the small windows with a sliding glass door and extending our deck so that we could sit outside with our coffee or tea, enjoying the tranquility of the space.

We were fortunate to find a contractor with a vision and started renovations with the kitchen. Rich traveled back and forth to work with the contractor, but most of the renovations happened while we were in California. Within a year, Rich's sister decided the Cape wasn't her place, and, with some creative financing, the house became ours.

Over the next few years, either Rich or I traveled to the Cape for short stays and to oversee renovations. We turned the recreation room into our living room, tearing out the paneling and the fireplace that sat opposite the pond, lowering the windows, and repositioning our furniture to take full advantage of the view.

Rich needed to stay close to the Bay Area to watch over his father in assisted living and to see clients, and I was busy teaching two groups and several students there. The added responsibility as well as desire to spend more time on the Cape gave me the courage to let go of one of my groups. As painful as it was to say goodbye to my fellow teachers and students, it was an important first step in finding balance in my life.

In January 2009, I spent a month completely alone in the Cape house. Mike was in Florida and Moe was working full-time in Boston. I'd yet to meet any neighbors, most of them gone for the winter anyway. It was as close to being at Gampo Abbey as I'd come since my retreat three years prior. I exhaled into the space, expecting nothing of myself other than to follow my whims. Most mornings began with meditation and a walk on Hardings Beach. Much like life at Gampo Abbey, I needed to forage for food, but in Chatham, I had grocery stores close by. I kept meals simple, sometimes indulging in prepared foods from the Chatham Village Market. Rather than letting a clock dictate my movements, I let my body tell me when it was time to eat and sleep.

Life wasn't completely carefree. I had a seminary retreat to teach in Connecticut at the end of the month, so some days I would study the transcripts and prepare outlines. Perhaps because I was teaching about Space, or because I was so relaxed, preparation didn't feel like work. I studied when I felt moved to study, much like I ate when I felt moved to eat. I dropped into my own natural rhythms like I had at Gampo Abbey.

After a week of watching birds flitting in the trees, I bought two bird feeders at the Bird Watchers General Store in Orleans and hung them on the deck. Endless hours passed as I watched the birds' comings and goings, and filled and refilled the feeders. I also bought a book and CD on backyard birds for the area so that I could identify my visitors and learn their language.

One day I spotted a great blue heron sitting on the opposite edge of the pond. I grabbed my binoculars and watched as he stood still for a long time, waiting for his next meal. I was completely absorbed, so much so that I felt like I was *inside* his skin and feathers. It reminded me of the experience I often had while sitting with students, not just perceiving them from a distance, but directly sensing their inner experience. It's a capacity called empathic sensing that develops as one becomes more transparent and receptive, a kind of "taking in" of the experience of the other. I was used to feeling this kind of sensitivity with students, my husband, and friends but had never experienced it with a bird.

I put down my binoculars and sat in this state, becoming one with the heron, solitary, unto myself. I felt the whistling wind, the hint of chill around my ankles, the freezing rain and gray clouds and black water and dark blue of my wings. The stillness was breathtaking.

I started spending longer stretches at the Cape house, sometimes using the time alone to prepare teaching retreats for the seminary or the Boston group. I dabbled in writing, something I had always wanted to do. For years I'd made excuses for not writing—too busy, who cares what I have to say, I can't.

When my friend Sandra invited me to join a memoir writing group with her, I said yes without thinking where it might take me. Like with meditation early on, I had resisted following my heart and instead let my mind run the show. But I was ready now, to live a life that felt more authentic. In time, writing, like meditation, became a spiritual practice as well as an enjoyable pursuit. And the Cape house was the perfect spot to practice both.

After Rich retired and his father died in 2015, we began to rethink our living situation. With more time away from the Bay Area, I resigned from most of my teaching responsibilities in California and shifted my focus to online mentoring of teachers and teachers-in-training. In 2014, I began teaching a Diamond Approach retreat group that met in Connecticut twice a year, and occasionally guest taught at the European seminary and groups in Germany. Being on the East Coast was making more sense than living in California. The air, the light, the foliage was what I grew up with, and I would have to wrench myself away when it was time to return home. Rich, on the other hand, grew up in Southern California, so the Cape was still a novelty.

Watching the sun rise over the pond each morning, bird songs the only sounds to interrupt the stillness, felt idyllic. The house renovations were complete, and we'd made new friends thanks to our puppy, Zoey, who stopped to say hello to everyone we passed on our walks in the neighborhood. Rich, who had played guitar much of his adult life, joined a group of musicians who met each Thursday to jam together. We hosted often, filling our home with wonderful music and good people. We had sold our home in San Rafael and were renting a house in Fairfax while deciding our next move.

One summer morning sipping coffee on the deck of our Cape house, we looked at each other and asked the obvious question: Why weren't we living here all the time? Other than harsh New England winters and some close friends in California, we couldn't come up with a good reason. In March 2016, we moved ourselves and our two-year-old Havanese puppy and became year-round residents of Cape Cod. It turned out to be a winter of record snowfall. Several inches dropped from the sky for days on end, and shoveling snow became a daily practice, along with meditation and writing.

Living full-time down the street from Mike and Moe meant spending more time together and deepening our bonds. While Moe worked in Boston during the week, Mike and I carved out time for just the two of us. We were both writing memoirs, he more rigorously than me, having retired from his private practice two years earlier. We were each other's first readers since we began writing, sending pieces back and forth by email, editing and brainstorming and supporting each other in our writing.

Now that we were neighbors, we scheduled writing days, usually at Mike's house in his favorite room, which we fondly called "the pond room." It had large picture windows overlooking Trout Pond, a wall of books, Mike's desk, and a display case of treasures he'd collected over the years. A huge brass statue of Lord Rama the Archer guarded the room from a corner window. Facing the pond was an L-shaped sofa and a chair with a pillow that said "Love you the most."

Mike sat on the long L of the sofa, his stack of books and computer nearby, with Jack, his cat, pushed up against his hips. I sat on the other end of the sofa with pillows behind me, legs stretched out in front, my toes touching Mike's leg while we wrote and read to each other. On World AIDS Day, December 1, 2016, Mike published *The Sea Is Quiet Tonight,* a memoir about his lover, who was one of the first men in Massachusetts to die of AIDS in 1984. I was Mike's sidekick at various book events, taking photos, selling books, and cheering him on.

Rich, Mike, and I spent time together, too, during the week. I often made dinner for the three of us, and we had lively conversations about music, books, and spirituality. It was at one of those dinners that we decided to do regular inquiries together, the main practice of the Diamond Approach. We took turns meeting at our house or Mike's, lighting a candle and meditating for a few minutes together to get centered. Then each of us took fifteen minutes to inquire into wherever we were, whatever we were experiencing, while the other two listened silently. Each inquiry was followed by five minutes of feedback, which might include asking questions if something wasn't clear or sharing how we were affected by each other's inquiry.

We called ourselves Total Beans, a play on *Total Being,* one of the more advanced teachings in the Diamond Approach. It's not easy to explain. A quote from Hameed from his book *Runaway Realization* captures the essence of it.

Total Being refers to the sheer indeterminacy of reality—to its nonexclusivity and its noncontainability . . . it is not defined by any particular experience; however, every experience expresses it . . . when we recognize that we are Total Being, what we usually sense is freedom . . . recognizing that we are Total Being is a maturation of realization.

Knowing that we can be anything, not just our personality, not just any one essential state or dimension, that we can be any emotion we are experiencing, nothing excluded, is what allows true freedom. Similar to One Taste, it's what every spiritual student is seeking, freedom to be completely what we are. I'm not sure who came up with the name, but calling ourselves Total Beans always made me smile.

Most weekends the four of us shared a meal together, usually at our house, sometimes at a restaurant. Mike, who was a wonderful chef, lost interest in cooking and to my chagrin, lived on Lean Cuisine during the week. Some Sundays, the four of us went to breakfast at Hangar B and then took a long walk on Hardings Beach. If I was teaching or Rich and I were traveling, we'd get back into the flow of our routine as soon as we were all together on the Cape. The longest breaks in seeing each other happened when Mike, who hated the snow, took off for Florida for six weeks in the winter. We stayed in touch with daily emails, but it never felt quite the same when Mike was gone.

Soon after my seventy-second birthday, I decided to take a sabbatical from teaching. I'd had one job or another since I was twelve years old, starting with babysitting. As a professional, my days were scheduled well in advance, initially with psychotherapy clients and later with private students and teaching retreats. I wanted to see what it was like to wake up to a completely blank calendar.

The idea of not working was both exciting and scary. By then I was collecting Social Security but would need to rely on Rich to carry most of our household expenses. That meant facing my aversion to asking for help, much like I had when I closed my psychotherapy practice to teach full-time. I worried that I might feel like I was wasting my time. Take care of myself and not my students? It sounded selfish and indulgent to my workaholic ears.

And then there was the issue of saying goodbye to yet another group of teachers and students that I loved. Over the past five years, John, my codirector, and I had created something special—not only a new Diamond Approach group but also a crucible to mentor newly ordained teachers. I had to ask myself the hard question: Why did I keep leaving groups after putting in the hard work of orienting students? And it *was* hard work! In the same way that was true for me when I joined the Diamond Approach, students would arrive with fixed ideas and concepts not only about who they were but about what it meant to become realized. Those ideas were deeply entrenched, and it took months and years of inquiry to penetrate the mind and discover reality free of misconceptions.

Did it have something to do with my attachment issues? Was I acting out my abandonment issues, leaving before I got kicked out or became irrelevant? Certainly, that was in the mix but not the whole story. The answer came during an inquiry with a fellow teacher and close friend. Sherry knew my patterns, both strengths and weaknesses. She told me the story of her friend who had a similar pattern but who didn't see it as a problem.

"You're a midwife," Sherry said, "just like my friend. You have a gift of translating complex spiritual concepts into language that's approachable. You navigate students through the birth canal and then once they can stand on their own two feet, your work is done."

I began making plans to step down from teaching. I taught the Connecticut group through 2019 and both the US and European seminaries. It made for a very full but satisfying prelude to my sabbatical.

When COVID-19 hit, I was ready to isolate. Finally, with just a handful of teachers to mentor, I could take some space for myself. Or so I thought.

CHAPTER TWENTY-NINE

Apocalypse

On a sunny morning in late May 2020 on Cape Cod, the forsythia bushes, harbingers of spring with their bursts of bright yellow, were fading. Lilacs had begun flowering, infusing the air with their strong, sweet scent. As Mike and I began a three-mile walk around our neighborhood, we commented on how, even though the trees were leafing out, they seemed less vibrant this year. Driveways were filled with cars. Summer residents had returned early from Florida to escape the pandemic. It was now entering the third month, and we wondered if it would ever end.

To neighbors familiar with us, we must have seemed engaged in our usual banter. We'd already exchanged early morning emails, our daily habit of sharing whatever was on our minds. How could they know that what we were discussing was the three-inch mass that had recently been discovered on Mike's left lung? I don't think they noticed how his breathing became more labored when we hit the inclines. But I did. I watched him occasionally hold his rib to manage the pain he had since January. It was getting worse, not better.

Our friendship had deepened over the decades, as together we weathered failed love affairs, the AIDS epidemic, deaths, and divorces. We celebrated too: his sobriety, our successful psychotherapy practices, me becoming ordained as a spiritual teacher, the publication of his memoir, and the joy of finally landing in happy marriages.

Our hope that one day we'd live on the same street had come to pass. Here we were, forty-five years later, with only four houses separating his front door from mine. What we hadn't imagined was that ten years after my husband and I bought our house on the Cape, Mike and I would be standing on Mike's porch, six feet apart, talking about death.

"I never thought of myself as someone who would get cancer," Mike said. The hospital wasn't scheduling nonessential procedures because of the pandemic, and without a CAT scan he didn't know the nature of the mass. But a mass of any size is scary.

"Me either. Heart failure or dementia but not cancer," I said. "Maybe it's just a buildup of congestion. The doctor *did* say that was a possibility, right?"

"Yes, or maybe I'm dying."

When either of us was facing adversity, we threw our arms around each other, offered words of sympathy, and then made a joke. He'd bend his six-foot-three-inch frame, and I'd reach up to meet him on tiptoes. We'd look into each other's eyes and say, "Oh well," our shortcut way of surrendering to the inevitable. We liked to pretend that we'd had the nerve, in younger days, to tattoo that phrase on the inside of our left wrists. Sometimes we wouldn't bother with the words, instead tapping the imaginary tattoo with two fingers.

But that was under normal circumstances, and now nothing was normal. Not in the world and not with Mike.

"To hell with social distance," I said, and reached out to hug him. He briefly sobbed. I did too, and then we stepped six feet apart again.

"I keep hoping that I'll wake up one of these mornings and realize it was a bad dream," Mike said.

"Me too."

Despite millions of moments of counting breaths while sitting in meditation, and days on end contemplating impermanence at Gampo Abbey fourteen years ago, my mind fragmented at the news of Mike's mass in his lung. *What if it* is *cancer? Or metastasized? Or inoperable, and he has only months to live?* For years we thought of ourselves as twin souls. We marveled almost daily, about the similarities of our experiences, from the profound to the mundane. If I'd had a bad night, it would not surprise me to read an early morning missive from Mike about his sleepless night. If Mike was happy for no apparent reason, so was I.

Our ponds were separated only by a road that ran between them. I liked to imagine that at one time they were the same pond, pickerel and trout swimming together among the snapping turtles and lilies. Like Mike and me, different yet the same.

I simply could not imagine a life without Mike in it.

Oh my God. We're twin souls. What if I've got cancer too? I thought about the mammogram I'd just scheduled and started to feel anxious.

I stood at the top of my driveway, taking in the beauty of Pickerel Pond. A pair of hooded mergansers were diving for fish. Cardinals, tufted titmice, and a host of other birds were singing their hearts out, in the throes of mating. The orioles and hummingbirds had just returned after the long winter. I was in a panic, wanting to shut down to ward off the frightening thoughts flooding my mind.

Can you just be in this *moment, Rose?*

If ever there was a time to stay present, it was now. I took some deep breaths and sensed myself. Within moments, I felt the familiar rush of warmth. I was back in my body. Disparate thoughts dissolved into a singular sense of presence. I reminded myself that reality is reality and resisting it is futile.

When I resumed walking down my driveway, it was at a slower pace, feeling the substantiality of my body and the quieting of my mind. I listened to the birds while gazing at the pond. I knew from experience that pulling back from pain was not the answer and vowed to keep my heart open to whatever came next.

That night I dreamed that the world was ending and that everything I had planned to do in the future was pointless. Out of habit, I started to make a list of groceries before realizing that I wouldn't need food. I wasn't scared but was having difficulty accepting that it really was the end. I kept slipping into old habits, thinking of something else I should do and then stopping myself. Forgetting and remembering.

When I awoke, the dream hung over me like a cloak I couldn't shake off. I reflected on the truth of the dream, that every moment is new, the old one dead and gone. How often I'd forget and act as if I could count on things happening the way I'd planned.

The following week, as I was taking Zoey out for her morning walk, Moe drove by with Mike in the passenger seat. They were both wearing baseball caps pulled low on their heads. Mike was looking uncharacteristically straight ahead. Moe rolled down the window and said they were on their way to the emergency room because Mike was having difficulty breathing.

As they drove away, I stood in the street, immobilized with fear, until Zoey tugged her leash as if to say, *hey, what about me?* I spontaneously started chanting Om Mani Padme Hum, the chant of compassion, both for Mike and to steady my own nerves. Mike spent the night in the hospital and was released the next morning, having finally gotten a CAT scan.

After being referred to a pulmonologist, Mike scheduled a PET scan for the following week. Moe was in Boston, so I drove Mike to the community college for the required COVID test prior to getting the scan. The next day, with a negative result in hand, I drove him to an outpatient clinic for his PET scan. Mike continued having difficulty breathing but we carried on, afterward stopping by Dunkin' Donuts for his large coffee, then driving to Hardings Beach. He was too tired to walk, so we sat on a bench while he drank his coffee, marveling at the beauty of the cloud formations in the bright blue sky. He was obsessed with clouds.

"If I die, I'll find a way to visit you. Look for me in the clouds."

I squeezed his hand as we took in the tranquility of the sky and sea. We'd both read a book by Cynthia Bourgeault, *Love Is Stronger Than Death,* about her close relationship with a monk and how they stayed in touch after he died. We wondered if we could do it too and how we might recognize the communication. But those conversations were theoretical. We didn't really think we were going to die.

A week later I was clearing out piles of papers in my office, enjoying the feeling of control over something if only my own messes, when Mike phoned. His pulmonologist had just called with results of the PET scan.

"Can you come down right now? It's really bad."

"I'm on my way," I said as I slipped into my shoes and ran out the door.

Sense.

Breathe.

Mike was waiting for me in the doorway of the pond room. He wasn't wearing his mask, but I was, more to protect him than myself. Mike could ill afford to contract the virus with his compromised lungs. I took his hand and we walked together to the couch. Uncharacteristically, he sat in the middle of the sofa, usually my spot, and I pulled up a chair to face him. Once we were at a safe distance, I took off my mask.

"It's really bad, Rose," he repeated, perhaps trying to absorb the severity of his situation. "Stage four inoperable lung cancer that's metastasized to every bone in my body. That's why I've been in so much pain."

I was stunned. Mike was stunned. It's one thing to imagine possibilities and another to face the facts. We started to cry, reaching at the same time for the box of tissues on the table between us. Impulsively I lit his meditation candle that always sat in the middle of the table. Buying time, searching for the right words. None came.

"I'm so sorry," I said, feeling the inadequacy of my response. I'd gone numb. Full on freeze mode.

"Did Dr. Spillane say anything about prognosis or treatment?" I asked.

"Moe and I meet with the oncologist next week," Mike said. "The good news is that the cancer isn't in any of my organs. He told me I was a very healthy man with a bad diagnosis."

Mike's voice had gone flat, matching my state. In a monotone, he told me he was hoping to qualify for immunotherapy.

"It's less toxic than chemo. No hair loss," he said. "I hate the idea of being nauseous and losing my hair."

"I hate all of it. I still can't believe this is happening to you."

"Me either," Mike said.

Where was my outrage that this was happening to my best friend, my soulmate? If I could have felt what I was truly experiencing, I might have had a temper tantrum. Or thrown my arms around him and told him he simply could not die. But in my state of shock, I had no access to my emotions.

As I walked home, it felt like the apocalypse. COVID had turned large metropolitan hospitals into war zones. Sea levels were rising, wildfires were destroying acres of land. And now this, a reality I had never imagined and felt ill-prepared to face.

CHAPTER THIRTY

Sharing Cancer with My Soulmate

A week after Mike received his diagnosis, we sat together on the couch in the pond room while he filled me in on the news from the oncologist. Six months prognosis if he did nothing. Maybe one to two years if chemo was effective. We discussed treatment options, including doing nothing, and how healthy he was despite the cancer. Moe, a nurse, was optimistic about chemo, and Mike was leaning in that direction. I was less optimistic, having watched my mother-in-law try chemo once and then shift to hospice after she was diagnosed with lung cancer. Her doctor encouraged her to make memories during the time she had left, which turned out to be exactly six months. She had a good life and a good death, and I wanted that for Mike.

But this was Mike's decision alone to make.

"Next step is to have a port inserted in my chest for chemo and a catheter inserted below my lungs to remove the buildup of fluids," said Mike.

"Sounds painful," I said, feeling as animated as a piece of plastic.

"It might be, and you know how I hate pain, but at least I'll be able to breathe more easily. Isn't it ironic that my worst fear is drowning and now I feel like I'm drowning every minute? A lot of good those swimming lessons are doing me now." Mike's lover, Mark, who had died of AIDS in 1984, was a sailor. Though terrified of water, Mike learned to swim so that he could join Mark on his boat.

"Ironic? Just a tad," I said before we both burst out laughing as we pointed to our imaginary tattoos.

"I feel so much better," Mike said. "You're the best."

"No, you're the best."

"We're lucky to have each other," Mike said as I got up to leave.

We were both doing our best not to get swept away by the undertow of fear and dread.

"Can I ask you a favor?"

"Anything," I said. And I truly would have done anything for Mike, anything to stave off my feelings of helplessness.

"Can you make me some of your polenta with parmesan cheese? My appetite isn't so good and that might jump-start it."

"In a heartbeat," I said as I hugged him goodbye.

As Mike prepared for his first round of chemo the following week, I drove to the outpatient clinic near my home for my mammogram, which had been postponed for a few months due to COVID. I'd never missed a year for the past thirty, but this one felt different. And not just because of the sterile environment once I stepped inside the front door of the clinic: having my temperature taken, everyone masked and keeping their social distance, hand sanitizers around every corner. Standing in front of the machine in my faded johnny, the most tender part of my body about to be squeezed between two ice-cold plates of steel, all I could think about was that I might have cancer too.

As I was leaving, the technician told me not to be concerned if I got called back for another scan. "It happens all the time," she said. I'd never been called back in the past or had a follow-up scan. I was certain that she'd seen something worrisome, so it wasn't a complete surprise when I was called the next week and told to go to the Cuda Breast Center. After a second mammogram, an ultrasound, and finally a biopsy, I was given the diagnosis: Stage one cancer in my left breast, invasive but not aggressive.

Within two weeks of each other, Mike and I had both been diagnosed with cancer.

The call back from the breast center came while I was in the middle of a haircut, having impulsively decided to have my hair straightened. I hardly recognized myself in the mirror, which added to my shock when the nurse suggested I stop by on my way home rather than giving me the results over the phone.

Once we were seated in her office, the nurse reassured me that I had a good prognosis, that it wouldn't be an easy road but that my cancer was highly treatable. I felt myself shut down as we discussed lumpectomy versus mastectomy and then set up appointments with a breast surgeon and an oncologist. I chose Mike's oncologist. It seemed somehow right.

I had promised Mike that I'd call him as soon as I got the results of my biopsy. After phoning Rich, I headed to Mike's house.

"God, Rose, what happened to your hair?"

"I had it straightened, to brighten things up. A bit extreme, no?"

"A bit," he said with a wry smile. "Now tell me about the biopsy."

I repeated what the nurse had told me, and her assurance that with surgery and radiation, I'd be fine. Mike teared up and I handed him a tissue. I remained dry-eyed, still numb, an old habit I'd picked up living with my unpredictable and sometimes volatile mother. And given what Mike was facing, my diagnosis didn't feel like a big deal.

"A lumpectomy, probably day surgery. And how bad can radiation be if I even need it?"

"It can be bad," Mike said. "I hate the thought of you going through this. Of *us* going through this. Can you believe we both have cancer?"

"Honestly, no."

"And your hair isn't helping," said Mike.

"I'm going to wash it when I get home. What a waste of time and money."

"Well, at least you have hair. I start chemo next week."

"Aren't we a pair? Facing cancer and worrying about our looks."

We touched our imaginary tattoos and laughed.

Mike was so weak that he now needed a walker to get from room to room, and the future looked grim. But in that moment, I was buoyed by our shared sense of humor and unshakable bond. We'd need both to navigate the coming weeks.

Though I vowed to stay present and keep my heart open, it proved challenging. My mind felt like the inside of a pinball machine. I walked Zoey, meditated with Rich, and cooked meals, activities that gave my days focus. Much like many others' response to being homebound by COVID, I became obsessed with *New York Times* recipes, trying out new ones every other night. Rich was thrilled, and I was grateful for the activity. Cooking had always been a pleasure. Now it felt like a necessity to keep me grounded.

Moe took a leave of absence so that he could take care of Mike. But he didn't know how to boil an egg, let alone prepare a meal. I made polenta and healthy broths for Mike, even though he had little appetite, and packed up meals for Moe a few times a week.

Before Mike started chemotherapy, we emailed each other daily. It was a practice for me, like meditation, to contemplate where I was and what was happening internally for me and then share it with Mike. But as Mike's ability to read or respond to my emails became more sporadic, I felt a hint of what was to come. The essence of our relationship slipped away weeks before he left his body, even though I didn't realize it until his emails stopped showing up in my inbox.

Prior to Mike's illness, I thought I'd made my peace with loss. One of the essential doctrines of Buddhism is impermanence, which saturates every aspect of life. All relationships end in death or separation. Loss is inherent to living, and so meditation becomes a practice of letting go, letting go of each breath on the exhale, opening to the next breath on the inhale, holding on to nothing. And when we do try to hold on, we suffer. *Resistance is futile.* I could suffer or surrender.

I did both. I took comfort in lighting a candle and a stick of incense. I took comfort in chanting, which seemed to quiet my mind. Meditation became a practice of watching my mind spin out, coming back to my belly or breath, settling for a few moments, and then spinning out again. I taught my students that there's no such thing as a "bad" meditation. I assured them that as long as they put their butt on the cushion or chair and made their best attempt to tame the mind, it was as valuable an experience as a meditation that opens into pure awareness.

But some days I suffered, giving myself a hard time for not being able to stay centered. Or giving in to my fear, imagining Mike suffering and dying and leaving me behind. Oddly, I wasn't frightened by my own cancer. In fact, I hardly thought about it. We were in the midst of a horrific pandemic, and my best friend was facing death. My cancer struck me as inconsequential. Perhaps I didn't have the resources to deal with it given the suffering I was seeing in the world and down the street. More likely I was in denial, titrating Reality to keep my head above water.

As much as I relied on the teachings of the Diamond Approach and Buddhism, I found myself falling back on my Catholic roots for comfort. I added my mother's crystal rosary beads to my altar and moved between chanting and praying. Teresa of Avila's prayer became a constant.

Let nothing disturb you,
Let nothing frighten you.

It was a reminder of the indestructibility of our essential or True Nature, which I'd come to know through the Diamond Approach. When I felt fear, I would sense into my heart. Yes, there was relative suffering, but the absolute truth was that I knew and felt love and the basic goodness of the universe permeating everything. Sometimes I had to step way back to reconnect with that realization, but it was always there when I was able to abide in my heart.

CHAPTER THIRTY-ONE

A July to Remember

Five days of Mike feeling energized after his first round of chemo gave us five days of hope. But the tumor continued to slough off fluid faster than the visiting nurse could drain it, and Mike was in a constant state of gasping for air. After another trip to the emergency room, he needed an oxygen tank hooked up to his nostrils. He dragged around the tank, grousing about the indignity of it, but also feeling relief from the terror of drowning.

Next came the purchase of a La-Z Boy–like chair that went up and down with the touch of a button. Mike and Moe had exquisite taste in furniture and art, and the dull gray chair was an eyesore. But it was the only place Mike could find relief from the pain wracking his body. He began to sleep in the chair rather than trying to lie down in bed.

July 1, Mike's birthday, had for years been a time to celebrate both Mike and the Fourth of July. I made my potato salad, Rich grilled, and Moe ordered an ice cream cake from the Ice Cream Café. Most times, friends or family joined the party; rarely was it just the four of us. The only question was how big of an ice cream cake to order and what flavors to include, ice cream being everyone's favorite dessert.

But this year Mike couldn't come to our house, both because of his pain and being hooked to an oxygen tank. We invited Anne, a friend of ours who knew and loved Mike. When her husband was in his last months, Mike had spent a few evenings visiting with him, giving Anne a much-needed break from caretaking. Even though it wasn't a summer meal, Mike asked me to make polenta with Bolognese sauce. He was hoping the familiar smells would spark his appetite.

Moe had set the dining room table, but Mike was too uncomfortable to move from his chair. Instead, we filled our plates and gathered around him in the living room. When I offered him a tiny bowl of food, he declined and said he'd wait for ice cream. Conversation was stilted, as we did our best to create a celebratory mood. No one was feeling anything but sorrow as we sat with our dear friend, a nasal cannula delivering oxygen to his emaciated body. We talked about ice cream—our favorite flavors, cone versus cup, what flavors were in the ice cream cake that was softening on the kitchen counter. It was the only subject that felt safe.

When Moe brought in the cake with candles, something was strange. They were fake! Thank goodness he was a nurse and knew better than to light a candle near an oxygen tank. We sang a subdued happy birthday and made Mike swear he'd be around next year. I remember looking into his eyes that knew the truth, even though neither of us wanted to face it.

The next three weeks were a series of trips to the emergency room and one hospital stay of three days to manage Mike's pain and breathing difficulties. Moe stayed by Mike's side, but no one else could visit due to COVID. I felt Mike slipping further away, our contact reduced to short phone calls and a few visits when he was home.

It was during our last visit on July 23 that Mike told me he was ready to die. Barely two months to the day of his diagnosis. Chemo wasn't working, and he wanted to stop but was concerned that Moe would be upset. I encouraged him to have the conversation with Moe, who I knew loved him and would support whatever Mike decided.

When Mike was hospitalized with pneumonia a few days later, I was able to reach him by phone for a brief conversation. He was ready for hospice and had spoken with Moe, who was supportive and assured Mike that he wouldn't die in the hospital. While Moe worked out transportation details, Rich went to their house to accept delivery of a hospital bed. Mike was transported home in an ambulance later that day so that he could die facing his beloved treed backyard and pond.

It was late July, and the sun was rising over the pond. Already 85 degrees, it was going to be a muggy one. Dawn was Mike's favorite time of the day. Mine too. Prior to cancer, by 5:30 in the morning, Mike would be stepping into his hot tub, and I would be at my desk writing and sipping a cup of tea. We loved waking before the sun, before the birds, before our partners, no matter the season. It was our time to be alone, to meet the world on our own terms.

I had fallen asleep in the clothes I'd been wearing for two days, white crop pants and a faded turquoise T-shirt with the inscription *Sagittarius: I'm usually right.* I needed a shower, but it would have to wait. Familiar with the signs—waxy skin, fingers curling in, breathing slowing down—I had watched death creep into Mike's pores. Rich and I kept a vigil while Moe slept for a few hours on the couch. When Moe awoke at midnight, I went home to get some rest.

I was in a fugue state, not thinking I wanted to be there when Mike died, or I didn't want to be there when he took his last breath. As I walked home, I wondered how it would feel if I missed his final moment. I remembered someone telling me that sometimes people choose to die when their loved ones have left the room. If we do have a choice about the moment of death, I was leaving the decision up to Mike.

When the phone rang five hours later, I knew who was on the other end.

"He's gone," Rich said.

"I'll be right there."

As I hurried the four doors down the street to Mike and Moe's house, I was filled with elation. Where was this coming from? I had expected to feel devastated, which would come soon enough, but, in the moment, all I felt was relief for Mike and the end of his suffering. Anyone watching me might have thought I'd lost my mind as I skipped down the street and pointed to the sky, saying out loud, "Good job. You went just the way you wanted, quickly and quietly. Travel well, my friend."

I opened the door to the mud room. Two large oxygen tanks dominated the space usually filled with shoes and coats. Just inside the mud room, a mountain of papers covered the dining room table. On top was the schedule of meds. Moe had created one worthy of a hospital chart. He needed it, to stay on top of the morphine and Ativan and Tylenol and as a distraction to stave off the terror of losing his partner of over thirty years.

The kitchen counters were littered with used syringes and medicine bottles, the spoils of war. The stillness inside the house caught in my throat, like a film of cotton batting. I forced myself to take a deep breath, then continued back to the pond room.

When I entered, everything seemed the same. Moe was sitting to Mike's left holding his hand. Rich was on Mike's right, touching his leg. Both were bowed as if in prayer. I walked quietly toward my place at Mike's head, where I'd stood or sat the last three days, stroking his damp hair, holding his hand, whispering words of comfort and encouragement. *You're doing fine. Relax, relax. You're* my *teacher now.* He'd smiled at that one. I remembered when Mike was my student, how one of his pet greetings was "Hi, Teach."

I touched his cool skin and kissed his eyes. I'd never see those sparkly blues again. I think I cried. I don't remember. His body was covered in a navy flannel blanket with the words LOVE, PEACE, SERENITY, JOY in large white letters, a present from one of his friends. I stroked his forehead and placed my hand on his chest. He smelled of death, which is to say that his familiar scent, a mix of mustiness and fabric softener, was already fading. I caught a whiff of lavender from a candle Moe had lit. It was disorienting. Mike preferred beeswax candles and burned one every morning when he meditated. I knew the pond room and the rest of the house would eventually become Moe's. I wanted that for him, but not yet.

The arrival of the visiting nurse was jarring. She wasn't the hospice nurse who had been coming daily since Mike's discharge from the hospital. This one was more of a Florence

Nightingale–type hell-bent on cheering us up. In a bright sing-song voice, she said all the wrong things.

"At least he's not suffering."

"He's at peace now."

Moe and I exchanged glances but were careful not to roll our eyes.

I wanted to push in her face and tell her to stop talking like he was dead. I refused to look at her. I didn't want to look at Mike's body either and focused instead on the hummingbirds sucking nectar from the mimosa tree in the side yard.

The undertakers arrived an hour later, wearing black suits, white shirts, and sympathetic eyes above their COVID masks. They seemed so young for the job but went about their business efficiently. Moe was clear that he didn't want to watch them roll Mike out in a bag, so Rich took Moe upstairs while I greeted the undertakers and showed them back to the pond room. I wanted to watch, hoping that it would shake me into reality. Instead, my eyes remained dry as a desert while the gurney was wheeled out the side door.

The next morning, I woke early, my first thought being that I needed to tell Mike what had happened. "You died," I wanted to say, "and it was a good death. But it happened too quickly."

It was the first of many mornings I forgot, only to remember again that Mike was gone. Despite the poet Rumi's urgings to stay awake, I wanted to go back to sleep rather than face a day without him. How was it that I was so unprepared? I knew he was dying for weeks. I was familiar with death, having buried both my parents, my husband's parents, my beloved godmother, and several friends. But nothing had prepared me for this kind of loss. Our lives were more deeply entwined than I had realized.

Over the next week, Rich and I stayed in close touch with Moe, whose days were filled with arranging for the removal of the hospital bed, oxygen tanks, and medical paraphernalia, as well as sending off death certificates to too many agencies and banks to count. It seemed inhumane, having to deal with so many strangers at this tender time. Moe said it was a relief to have things to do, but Jack the cat refused to leave the pond room. Like the rest of us, he was waiting for Mike to return.

CHAPTER THIRTY-TWO

Intermingling of Grief and Cancer

A week to the day after Mike died, Rich, with Zoey on his lap, dropped me off in front of the cancer wing of Cape Cod Hospital, the same wing Mike had visited too many times over the past few months. Halfway up the steps, I turned to wave, then walked through the front door. "It's only a lumpectomy," I said to myself, trying to stave off my growing anxiety. If not for COVID, Rich would have been walking next to me, holding my hand, assuring me he'd be right there in the waiting room as soon as I got out of surgery. I felt a profound sense of aloneness, which Mike, too, must have felt. "Don't let me die alone here," he'd begged Moe and me during his last hospitalization.

After changing into a johnny and having my vitals checked in pre-op, I was wheeled to another wing of the hospital so that the biopsy physician, with ultrasound as a guide, could insert a needle in my breast to mark the spot of the tumor. Mike was right. This was a bigger deal than I'd let myself imagine. The room was dark and cold, and I felt scared, especially when the doctor tented the needle to protect it from moving while I waited for surgery.

My older sister had breast cancer when she was fifty and, knowing how squeamish I am about such things, warned me about the needle. "It's the worst part of the whole procedure." I called her often to ask questions and share my anxieties because I knew she understood. At the time, I hadn't fully appreciated what she went through and vowed to be there for her if she ever needed me in the future.

Back in pre-op, I meditated to calm my nerves. Two hours passed as I watched patients come and go. The wait gave me an opportunity to focus on myself and the seriousness of my diagnosis instead of minimizing it in comparison with Mike's. With the exception of talks with my sister, I tried not to think of myself as a cancer patient. A precarious needle sticking out of my breast pierced the bubble of denial.

At 11:30, an hour past the time I had been scheduled for surgery, I felt the urge to pee. I rang for the nurse, who walked me to the bathroom, assuring me that the surgeon would be visiting soon.

"She's running behind, but she'll take her time with you too, when it's your turn."

I was relieved when the anesthesiologist finally wheeled me down some halls and into the operating room, which was small, brightly lit, but freezing. Why can't they keep a place where patients are half-naked more temperate? The surgeon reassured me that mine was a straightforward procedure as a nurse placed a warm blanket over my lower body. When the anesthesiologist instructed me to go to a relaxing place, I pictured myself on a private beach on Maui with turquoise waters and powdery white sand. I wondered if most patients picked the tropics, but before I could finish my wondering, I was out.

My next conscious thought, as I awoke in post-op, was that Mike was dead. It was as if someone had just announced the shocking news over the intercom. I let out a wail. A nurse sprang into action.

"On a scale of one to ten, how much pain are you in?" she asked from the foot of my bed. I shook my head, but she persisted.

"One to ten, just hold up your fingers." When I shook my head no again, she came to the side of my bed and injected something into a line attached to my arm.

"This will help with the pain," she said as she stroked my forearm.

"It's not that kind of pain," I managed to say.

Two weeks later, I started a month of radiation. As I pulled into one of the parking spaces marked "For cancer patients only," I hesitated, not sure if it meant me. Then I wondered if Mike had parked in that very space. Or maybe Moe, while he waited for hours for Mike to get a CAT scan or be evaluated for admission.

I fared as expected: fatigue, scorched skin, more fatigue. Because the tumor was in my left breast the heart needed to be protected, which meant I had to lie on my stomach, face in a cradle, my breast hanging through a hole in a metal plate. Sometimes I felt Mike's presence hovering nearby, which made me angry when it didn't make me miss him even more. *How could you have left me to deal with this alone?* When the three minutes of radiation ended, I reached for my mask hanging on the face cradle, wiped away tears, and walked back to the dressing room to slather my chest with Aquaphor, a healing ointment.

Friends offered to drive me, but I preferred being alone. Talking required more energy than driving. And it was a relief to grieve in private. Only three weeks had passed, but I was already telling myself it was time to get over it. I tried to read some books on grief that Rich recommended, but couldn't concentrate. Intellectually I knew it would take months, maybe even years, to process Mike's death. Emotionally I was acting and feeling just like most human beings do when they experience profound loss. Neither my spiritual practices nor my psychological training could save me from my feelings, and the last thing I wanted to do was dive into the center of them.

Though I've always prided myself on my independence, it wasn't my habit to isolate. When I tore ligaments in my knee skiing many years ago, I welcomed the friends who came to my rescue, bringing food and lugging a Christmas tree up two flights of stairs, then helping my son decorate it. And this time I deeply appreciated my book club buddies, smiles beneath their masks, who dropped off meals for me and Rich each day of the week after my lumpectomy. In fact, it was the high point of the day, discovering what delicious meal awaited us: chicken Marbella, Niçoise salad, paella. The women were generous and kind, yet I couldn't bring myself to do more than send thank-you texts, except for my closest friend on the Cape, Anne. Her husband had died the year before, and she knew how to be with me without expecting conversation.

I'd come home from radiation, pet Zoey, kiss my husband, eat lunch, and crawl under the covers for the rest of the afternoon. Though I'd been told to expect fatigue, I hadn't anticipated how debilitating it would be. It reminded me of the first few months of pregnancy, an irresistible fatigue that pervades every cell in the body. Rich fixed dinners, and we'd watch something easy on Netflix like *Jane the Virgin*. What a relief to lose myself in someone else's drama and have a few belly laughs. Though I fell into bed early, deep sleep was evasive. I woke at 1:00 a.m. unable to get back to sleep and then had to face another morning without Mike. Some days when the loss seemed unbearable, I wished I had died too.

As radiation came to an end, I craved the relaxation of that pristine beach I'd envisioned on the operating table. It was early fall, not beach weather on the Cape, but I wanted to sit in an Adirondack chair at the edge of Pleasant Bay, wrapped in blankets while the movement of waves and the breezes of salty air soothed my soul. We hadn't gone anywhere since the pandemic and had no plans to celebrate our anniversary. Rich, too, was restless for a change of scenery. We booked three nights at a local hotel, left Zoey with our dog sitter, and drove ten minutes to a cottage with unobscured vistas and direct access to the beach. Though I was still fatigued and spent afternoons napping and reading, the weather was perfect for early morning and late afternoon walks on the beach. We watched the sun rise and set, the tides come and go. The rhythms of nature worked their magic, coaxing me back into my body.

The night of our thirty-first anniversary, we bundled up and walked to our favorite restaurant, which offered outside dining. It had been seven months since we'd sat at a table other than our own or been served by anyone other than each other. It was a reminder of the pleasurable life we took for granted before COVID, before cancer, before death.

After a short week's respite, I began antihormone therapy to prevent a recurrence of cancer. Like many breast cancers, mine was hormone driven. I was anxious about the side effects, menopause redux. I read and reread the literature on Arimidex, knowing I'd be on it for five years if I could tolerate it. I anticipated mood swings, joint pain, and dry skin, but wasn't prepared for the intense fatigue or the nausea that came on after two days. Another reminder of the early days of my pregnancy. Back then I didn't mind enduring the discomfort, knowing that soon I would be a mother. But now I found myself under the covers most days. Rich was kind and patient, for which I will be ever grateful. He, too, was grieving the loss of his good friend. I wished I could be there for him but lacked the inner resources. He stroked my forehead, assured me that this, too, would pass, and encouraged me to contact Barbara, the therapist I'd worked with when we lived in California.

The double whammy of grief and cancer finally caught up with me, and I slid into a deep depression. I didn't want to talk to anyone, not even Rich. How was I going to find the energy to tell my story to Barbara? And how could she help anyway? She couldn't bring Mike back, and wasn't it about time to stop mourning anyway? Why was I acting like such a baby? Many people had far worse cancer stories than mine.

With gentle prodding from Rich, I reached out to Barbara. She helped normalize what I was feeling, encouraging me to give myself more time and space. "It's only been three months!" she reminded me. And it did help to talk, to get some perspective on what was happening to my body and psyche. Not only was I adjusting to Mike not being here, but I was also adjusting to decreasing hormone levels.

When I was able to surrender to my grief, things shifted. I added journaling to my daily meditation practice, reached out to my friends and sisters, and stopped chastising myself. The last thing the heart needs during painful times, during any time, is abuse. I replaced the harsh messages from my inner critic to get over it with compassion. *Rest. Cry if you feel like crying. Stay close to yourself.*

On the morning of the winter solstice, I awoke feeling like Persephone back from the underworld. Though we usually think of her rebirth in spring, I briefly returned to the land of the living on the darkest day of the year. The light in the sky seemed brighter, colors and shapes more vibrant. I looked around my house, taking in the beauty of what my husband and I had created over our years of living on the Cape. I watched Rich, in the kitchen, making his morning coffee. It was as if seeing him for the first time, and I was flooded with gratitude and love. I felt like a newborn, vulnerable and helpless and alive.

Mike and I shared a cancer diagnosis. I survived, and he didn't. We shared ponds too, mine Pickerel and his Trout, visible through the barren trees from my living room window. From that vantage point, they seemed like the same pond. Perhaps they really *were* one pond some fifteen thousand years ago when the glacier ice melted, leaving behind massive holes, or "kettles" that later filled with fresh water. Mother Nature creates and destroys and creates again. I had no choice but to continue life without Mike just down the road, but it was not a choice I was ready to embrace.

CHAPTER THIRTY-THREE

Grief's Many Faces

In early spring of 2021, nine months after Mike died, Moe and I started planning Mike's memorial. He had decided not to hold it following Mike's death, both because it was during the height of COVID and because he wasn't yet ready to face a memorial. Together we decided to hold one outdoors in July, between what would have been Mike's seventy-seventh birthday and the one-year anniversary of his death.

When Mike was turning seventy, he thought he'd like a large stone for the backyard to mark the event, but somehow the years went by, and no stone was purchased. It seemed fitting, then, when Moe decided to buy a rose quartz stone as a tribute to Mike. His plan was to put it in the lower garden, near the pond, and to dedicate it at the memorial.

When Moe told me he'd purchased the stone, I felt a twinge of irritation about not being included in the choice. In my imaginal mind, I was the widow and should have been consulted. I said all the right things. *How lovely. I can't wait to see it.* But I could wait, and I did wait, and it wasn't about not being consulted. I didn't want to see anything tangible reminding me that Mike was gone.

To get to the stone, I would have to walk into Moe's backyard, past the pond room where Mike and I had spent countless hours writing, talking, meditating, laughing. Where the white marble Buddha sat that screamed Mike, the Buddha he took with him when he went to Florida in the winter. I joked with him that it was like the flag over the Vatican: When it was raised, the pope was in residence; when the Buddha was in the window, Mike was home.

The Buddha remained, but Mike was gone, and the pond room was changing. Moe, the quintessential gardener, had already moved a plant into the room after Mike died, something Mike forbade. I was proud of Moe for claiming his own space in the home that Mike had dominated with his large presence. But the first time I walked into the room, to find the poem Mike had asked me to read at his memorial, I gasped. Mike's desk was still as he'd left it, the poem in a folder on top, and all his Buddhist icons on the desk or in the glass-fronted bookcase next to the desk. It still smelled like Mike, especially around the desk and his corner of the sofa, but even Jack the cat knew something had changed. Rather than curling up in his spot on the couch next to Mike, he was lying on the floor, next to his food bowl.

After Mike died, when I could barely tolerate his absence, I called Moe to ask if I could visit. We sat in the pond room, holding hands, talking about how we were both still in shock. I noticed the one plant Moe had moved into the room.

"There are more coming. I can tell," I said with some amusement.

"Yup, he might strike me dead, but I've always imagined this room filled with plants."

"It's OK," I said. And I meant it.

It was too painful to come into the house without Mike, but Rich and I took comfort in spending time with Moe. We invited him for meals during the week and started a ritual, *Saving Sunday*. Before COVID, going out to Hangar B for breakfast was a special treat. We'd be the first in line at 8:00 a.m. to avoid the after-church crowd. Now the restaurant was closed but offering takeout. We took turns picking up our food order and then sat around our dining room table, checking in with how we were faring. Each of us felt the loss of Mike in our own way. Some conversations were more somber than others, but Moe's sense of humor prevailed even in his grief.

Several months after Mike died, I got a call on my cell phone. The caller ID said Mike Ward. I freaked out and answered, not knowing what to expect. Nothing, empty silence. I hung up and called Moe to let him know. He said he had just tried to phone me but got my voicemail.

He also told me that he'd been trying to get Mike's name off the account and thought he had. I asked Moe to try calling me again. This time Moe's name appeared. Was Mike sending a message, letting me know he was around? Or was it just a Verizon glitch? I preferred believing that it was Mike's way of making contact. It took Moe a year to get Mike's name and number off the account, though I've yet to delete him from my contacts.

Eventually I visited the rose quartz stone near the edge of the pond. On a morning walk with Zoey, she pulled to go down the side yard of Moe's house, something she'd never done before. Reluctantly I followed, taking a quick glance at the Buddha in the window.

The stone was smaller but more beautiful than I had imagined. Moe had made a good choice. I touched the wet earth around it. I knew Mike wasn't there, but it made me feel a bit closer to him. I sat on a bench nearby, Zoey at my feet, and looked out on Trout Pond. How had this happened? And why? Mike and I were supposed to have years of living down the street from each other. He was the reason Rich and I moved to the Cape. I wondered if we'd stay, if I could tolerate living on the Cape without him, even though I couldn't imagine where we would go. Did I believe that if we moved, Mike's death would be less painful?

The sun was shining on the morning of the memorial, almost a year to the day after Mike died. The humidity was blessedly low and the air fresh after a rainstorm the night before. It was a pristine summer day, sky as blue as Mike's eyes. By this time, we had reunited with Gregg, and he was staying with us for the week. Gregg paid close attention to me the way Zoey had kept her eyes on me when I was recovering from cancer. Before he died, Mike asked Rich to play his favorite song, "I Shall Be Released," at the memorial. Rich was practicing in the living room while I fixed breakfast for the three of us.

An hour before guests arrived, Gregg picked up the food from the caterers and met Rich and me at Moe's. Moe had done a beautiful job of creating an environment that was both festive and poignant. On the patio just outside the French doors, he set up a table with photos of Mike and his family and friends. Next to the photos were a copy of Mike's book and programs for the memorial with Mike's photo from his memoir on the cover. I lingered, running my fingers gently over his face, willing him back to life.

Just below the patio, under a tent, was one long table for sandwiches and two for desserts. "Mike's AA buddies love their sweets," said Moe. The chairs were in rows facing the pond. Rich sat off to the side, playing soft guitar music as people arrived. Kim, the minister who had married Mike and Moe the day after gay marriage was legalized in Massachusetts, opened the ceremony by saying, "Mike didn't want to die." I watched his primary care physician, who was sitting in the first row of chairs, dissolve into tears. I knew she had come to love Mike, as did everyone he befriended, but I also wondered if she felt guilty about missing the clues along the way: that Mike was dealing with something more serious than GERD or a rib that was slow to heal.

Moe gave a moving eulogy and invited a few other people to speak. When it was my turn, I read the poem that Mike had saved from *The New Yorker* in 2003 by Jane Hirshfield. It begins with the line *Like a lover, your life bends down and kisses your life.*

Years of teaching helped get me through the reading without dissolving in tears.

After people shared, Moe and Kim led us to the rose quartz stone, where Moe scattered some of Mike's ashes. The rest he planned on taking to Omaha, if the pandemic ever ended, to be scattered on the graves of Mike's family. I looked out over the pond while Moe said a few words next to the stone. The water was perfectly still, reflecting clouds in the sky, which reminded me of Mike's words, "look for me in the clouds." I searched in vain as people turned to head back to the tables filled with sandwiches and sweets.

It was a day to get through, and I got through it. While a few people lingered on the lawn, Moe and I retreated to the kitchen to begin the cleanup. "Job well done, my friend," I said to Moe. We both knew it was not the end of anything, merely another step in the long process of grieving.

CHAPTER THIRTY-FOUR

Practicing Leaning into Life Again

When Mike died, it felt like the bottom dropped out, leaving me in a painful state of emptiness. I could no longer put pen to paper. I tried composing emails to close friends about what I was experiencing, but each time, I was flooded with the realization that my first reader and best friend was gone.

Meditation practice, the one thing that had always anchored me in spacious emptiness, was agonizing. My husband and I sat together most mornings, but when I'd close my eyes and sense myself, I'd start weeping. I didn't want to feel loss, yet loss permeated my consciousness. I had to remind myself over and over again to surrender, to let the tears come, to trust that beyond tears and loss was something more fundamentally true. On the rare days that I could access the depth and stillness of my deeper nature, my mood would briefly lift.

I descended into the underworld of the River Styx, mostly submerged, unable or unwilling to break the surface and return to the world of the living. I wanted to stay with my friend, hold on to him even if it meant the end of my life too. I experienced myself as an empty husk, easily buffeted by eddies and currents of the river, no sense of direction. Had I surrendered? Not really. I rejected the emptiness all the while longing for it, longing to be released from suffering. I went through the motions of daily life, a ghost moving among the living. The terrain reminded me of other times I'd felt abandoned: by my mother, when she was taken from me soon after my birth through no fault of her own, and again when she disowned me for marrying my first husband; by Mike back in the '80s when he stopped talking to me; by my son when he disowned me in the '90s.

To assuage my pain, I turned to nature, the only element in my environment that felt free of demands. My seven-year-old Havanese stayed close at hand. Zoey would tuck her body next to mine in the bed or on the sofa, nudge my legs as I moved from room to room as if to remind me of her constancy. Her attunement to my wordless state was soothing. It was Zoey I reached for when I couldn't reach for anyone else. I watched her closely, the way she watched me, for guidance on how to get through the day. She spent hours either napping or sitting at the sliding glass door that overlooks our pond, watching the trees swaying, the birds visiting our feeders on the back deck, the squirrels attempting to steal some seeds. She was content to simply sit and watch.

One sunny day in early June I decided to give Zoey's way a try. We sat on the deck together, she with her arms and legs splayed out on the warm wood, me on a chair, both of us facing the pond. Initially I noticed what I always noticed: birds coming to the feeders or flitting among the branches of the many oak trees in our backyard hill leading down to the water. The pond, clear and still, had a few ripples now and then as a fish came to the surface. When I relaxed my focus, the way I do in meditation, not trying to "see" anything, but rather allowing the colors and shapes, and the space in between shapes, to come to me, my perception shifted. With a softened gaze, more details appeared. Colors became more vibrant, the leaves silky green, the cardinals bright red, the pond a swirl of blues and greens and grays.

Nature was offering me guidance. No need to make an effort or push away or feel more deeply. Keep your heart open. Everything happens in its own time. No need for stories about loss, abandonment, weather. Life happens, death happens, simply, effortlessly. The oriole nest in the oak tree outside our living room window was empty, the fledglings exploring the neighborhood before heading south for the winter. They would return, late April, as they did each spring, and nourish themselves on my offerings of oranges and grape jelly. Autumn would come soon, turning leaves orange, red, and brown. In winter, the leaves would die and blanket the ground, leaving bare branches to weather the cold.

The last verse of a Vajra song came to mind.

Nothing to do,
nothing to force,
nothing to want,
and everything happens by itself.

As we approached July 30, the first anniversary of Mike's death, I was pulled back down by the undertow of grief. It didn't help that another friend of mine, a fellow teacher of the Diamond Approach, had just died of lung cancer. I attended her memorial on Zoom on July 21. Rich watched helplessly and wondered if I'd ever be myself again.

I wondered too. I thought about death a lot, and of the people I'd lost over the years. I remembered how palpable my mother's presence was after she died, how I had conversations with her now and then. I waited for Mike to show up, but he remained silent. His absence was devastating.

One Sunday morning I read an article in the *New York Times* "It's Never Too Late" column about a ninety-three-year-old woman, Vera Jiji. She picked up the cello at age sixty-two after hers sat in the closet for forty years. I started thinking about the piano, which I had played as a child. When I was thirteen, I begged my parents to let me stop lessons after performing Chopin's Nocturne in E-flat at a recital. I was terrified and managed to play the piece from memory, but I knew I never wanted to do that again.

I started reminiscing about piano and how much I had enjoyed it before the recital. When I mentioned this to Rich, he encouraged me to buy a keyboard to find out if it was something I still might enjoy. The day we unpacked and set up the keyboard, I felt excitement for the first time since Mike's illness. I ordered some music books online, copies of my old Michael Thompson books, hoping to relearn the Nocturne. It would take months of practice to return to that skill level, but I remembered how to read music and delighted myself by playing simple pop tunes. In time, I started working with a piano teacher who encouraged me to play what I loved, classical pieces like The Swan and Moonlight Sonata and eventually Chopin's nocturne.

I outgrew the keyboard within six months and started shopping for a piano. Again, with Rich's encouragement, I bought a beautiful Yamaha. I practiced a few hours each day, wishing my arthritic fingers could move more gracefully over the keys. But it didn't matter. What I was actually practicing was how to lean into life, and how to simply enjoy the activity of making music without pushing myself. It was a lesson from meditation, how to simply sit without expectations of having the perfect meditation. It's not so easy to let go of the need for perfection when raised by two perfectionists.

CHAPTER THIRTY-FIVE

In the World but Not of It

People say that the second year of grieving is the hardest. That's when you realize the missing person isn't coming back from a long vacation. The second July after Mike died was hell. I dropped into such a profound depression that I began to despair of ever fully recovering. I cried most days, both from the loss of my dear friend and more so from losing touch with myself. Only my spiritual practices gave me the strength to get through each day and some idea of how to work with my grief. I took deep breaths, reminding myself that the only way through it was by allowing it. But I was missing something more fundamental.

Once again, I reached out to Barbara, my Bodynamics therapist, to discuss the possibility of taking antidepressant medication. She had retired but made herself available by phone for emergencies. I told her about my depression and asked her advice about medication. To my surprise, she suggested I first watch a series on Netflix based on Michael Pollan's book *How to Change Your Mind*. Pollan reviews the history and use of psychedelics such as LSD, psilocybin, MDMA, and the

Native American sacred medicine of mescalin. Some amazing clinical trials had proved their efficacy in the treatment of psychological disorders until the United States, President Richard Nixon in particular, banned the scientific study of and use of psychedelics.

Though I had smoked my share of marijuana in the '60s and '70s, and Mike and I tried mushrooms a few times, I never viewed substances as anything other than recreational drugs. I had read about people who experienced LSD as a doorway to enlightenment. I was too scared to try it myself. I chose instead the path of meditation and inquiry and had already experienced expansive states of consciousness without the aid of drugs. I knew that what I was seeking was already within me.

The problem was that I couldn't access the stillness, depth, and clarity of my essential nature. It had been home base for me over the years of my involvement with Buddhist meditation and the Diamond Approach. The loss of contact with my depth was more devastating than the loss of any one person, even if that person had been a central figure in my life for decades.

Rich and I viewed the series together, and I felt a glimmer of hope as I watched various participants in the studies share how the drugs had an impact on them. Besides lifting serious depressions and other psychological problems, many of the participants had enlightenment experiences that eased their fears of illness and death. As I listened to them describe experiences of Oneness and interconnectedness, I wept. I knew these states intimately but felt disconnected from the immediacy of them in my consciousness.

And though my path has always veered slightly off what my parents would have perceived as the straight and narrow—marrying a Black man, studying Transactional Analysis instead of Freudian analysis, practicing spiritual psychotherapy before it became mainstream, becoming a Diamond Approach teacher instead of a teacher of any of the more well-known Buddhist traditions—I was anxious about trying earth medicine to deal with my depression.

As luck would have it, or more likely divine providence, I had lunch the next week with a friend of mine on the Cape who was a therapist and studying earth medicine. She was familiar with microdosing, which involves taking a small amount of psilocybin two or three times a week. She also participated in a medicine journey with a professional guide and was so impressed that she decided to become a guide herself. Over beet poke salads, she shared details of the yearlong training she had recently begun.

Psychedelics were illegal, but Meredith offered some of her psilocybin and coached me on how to microdose. An important step in the process is blessing the medicine and setting an intention. It sat on my desk for three weeks before I took my first dose. Though I used a very small amount and felt only slightly altered, I lay in my bed for an hour unable to do much of anything but sense my arms and legs. It may have been the first time I was truly still since my diagnosis and Mike's.

After a month of microdosing and noticing an uptick in my mood, I decided to embark on a guided journey. Meredith referred me to one of the premier guides in Massachusetts. Her knowledge and experience leading medicine journeys was impressive. Though costly, it was thorough. I participated in three exploratory sessions to acquaint Jacquelin with my psychological issues. Using primarily Internal Family Systems Therapy, a system that believes the mind is made up of relatively discrete subpersonalities, each with its own unique viewpoint, Jacquelin and I delved into my history as well as my spiritual background. By the end of these sessions, I knew intuitively that I could trust her and scheduled my journey.

In October, two years and three months after Mike's death, I arrived at Jacquelin's home, located in a bucolic setting on the outskirts of Boston. Along with her assistant, Sara, she walked me through a process of centering and setting my intention. My only intention was to reconnect to the depth of my being. I prayed to the four directions for guidance, took the medicine after blessing it, and entered a process that lasted five hours.

My years of psychological and spiritual exploration were good preparations to make the best use of the medicine. Rather than being frightened, the journey was a homecoming, a reunion with the Divine. Covered in a plush comforter, I settled into a mattress on the floor, with Jacquelin and Sara sitting nearby. With ambient music streaming through headphones, a boundless illuminated black expanse opened. The emptiness I'd been experiencing, which felt ominous and devoid of meaning, now enveloped me in a soothing blanket of soft velvet. I welcomed it—the spaciousness of True Nature—and surrendered to it completely. Much like in inquiry practice, insights arose spontaneously, bringing wisdom before disappearing back into the black abyss.

Similar to my realization at Gampo Abbey, I saw death more dispassionately, including Mike's. Death happens, and it's not an end of anything other than human life. I finally accepted that Mike was dead. I was alive and my life was here on earth. What remains of Mike and others close to me who have died is love. The love is always here.

An hour before the end of the journey, Jacquelin and Sara took turns sitting with me while the other prepared soup and snacks for us to eat afterward. The smell of food triggered a preverbal state of panic, of not getting enough sustenance, not trusting the milk. I remembered my issues with food and nourishment over the years: difficulty cooking for myself, feeling traumatized after teaching the essential aspect of Nourishment for the first time, working with Barbara on my abandonment issues. In my mind's eye, I saw the young child who could not, would not, surrender.

It was like watching a movie of the baby who refused the bottle, who was afraid of entrusting another to care for her. I watched her growing up and being slapped down whenever she asserted herself. I saw her confusion about love and power, a belief that she couldn't have both, couldn't *be* both.

And then my mother appeared as a young girl, suffering from her own traumas. I held her in my lap, comforting her as she wept. I understood how all the mothers in my lineage showed love through food. I felt appreciation for them and sorrow for my own reluctance to accept their expressions of love. All of this washed over and through me, cleansing me of hurts and sorrows related to nourishment, while being held in the arms of the Divine Mother.

During this process, I asked Sara if she would hold my hand. It was a profound moment for me, asking for help and taking in her unwavering support for what seemed like hours but was probably only fifteen minutes. She let me hold on for as long as needed. When I let go, I felt whole again and knew that whatever support I needed to live my life was already here. I could trust my instincts to know when and who to ask for support, and when to turn to myself, relying on my own inner resources.

It took weeks to process these insights and the various other experiences I had while on the medicine. Two integration sessions with Jacquelin and Sara helped, and I emerged feeling at peace with myself. I had the capacity again to meditate and to move through my life with awareness and presence.

The experience of the medicine journey was a returning, but not to the self I was before the pandemic or before Mike's death or before my cancer. The world had changed dramatically in three short years as a result of both COVID and climate change. And so had I. Grief and illness burned through vestiges of my historical self—the striving, the insecurity, the self-criticism—allowing more access to my truer self. It was reminiscent of the emptying out of my familiar self during my last week at Gampo Abbey.

Stepping back and seeing life more objectively, my own included, brought with it a renewed sense of freedom. In the world but not of it. Every mistake, every painful moment I thought I'd never live through, was as valuable as the many joyful experiences and expansive years of spiritual growth. Each passage of my life has been guided by a force beyond my egoic self. The many months when I doubted guidance and doubted the meaning of my life were simply misunderstandings. Mike's death was part of my own unfoldment, a vehicle of wisdom as well as a preparation for my own death.

Soon after Mike died, Moe gave me the talisman that Mike kept on his desk, a small stone with the word TRUST carved into its smooth surface. It sits now on my desk. I run my fingers over it each morning, invoking its guidance to gently touch those places in my soul that still doubt, still resist the current of my life. Is the work of a seeker ever done? I used to imagine a time when I could rest, not dig deeper, just be. Now I approach the dig as simply being myself, a lover of truth with a ceaseless curiosity about the mysteries of life and death.

Nothing to do,
nothing to force,
nothing to want,
and everything happens by itself.

Acknowledgments

This story was written and revised multiple times over the past ten years, and my heart is filled with gratitude for everyone who inspired, supported, and guided me along the way.

Mike, my best friend and first reader, never wavered in his belief that I could write this story. When he knew he was dying, he made me promise that I would complete it. Those deathbed wishes carry weight and without them, I might have given up.

I've been fortunate to meet some amazing writing teachers at workshops along the way—Joan Wickersham, Madeleine Blais, Martha McPhee, Hester Kaplan—and the incomparable Ann Hood, my mentor over the past several years. Thanks to Andre Dubus III, who, at a Writers in Paradise conference, implored me to stay in scene in a way that changed my writing. When I began writing this memoir, Mike introduced me to Ken Harvey, who became my first writing teacher. He has remained a friend and invaluable guide on this journey.

Thank you to dear friends, many of them authors, for taking time to read various iterations of this book and offer invaluable support and feedback: Anne LeClaire, Byron Brown, Celia Jeffries, Elizabeth Walker, Linda Novak, Marcia Wakeland, Moe Melchiono, Philippa Lubbock, Sandra Maitri, Sara Hurley, Sherry Anderson, and Wilderness Sarchild. Thanks also to Anne Singer, Jane Bronson, and Susan Weilly, teachers of the Diamond Approach whose wisdom and kindness I can always count on.

Deep gratitude for my life teachers: my mother, my son, my beloved students, Jack Kornfield, Hameed Ali, Jeanne Rosenblum, Lama Drimed, Lama Palden, and Dan Brown. I learned from each of them and carry those lessons in my heart. I owe what sanity I enjoy to Peter Tsantilis and Barbara Renshaw.

Thank you to the team at She Writes Press led by the amazing Brooke Warner, who guided me each step of the way as I navigated the process of publishing my first book. Everyone who tinkered with the manuscript, especially Sheila Trask and Celia Jeffries, made it a better read.

I am so fortunate to have my two sisters in my life. They knew me when and continue to love me anyway.

Deepest gratitude for Rich, my partner over the last thirty-five years. His steadfastness and love gave me the courage to open my heart fully and to follow my dreams. He graciously held down the fort while I traveled during my teaching years and again when I disappeared for days on end to write this book. He is my rock and, as I playfully remind him, my favorite husband.

About the Author

photo credit to Kim Roderiques

Rosanne Annoni was a successful psychotherapist for thirty-five years in the Bay Area before becoming an ordained teacher of the Diamond Approach in 2000. She has taught students and mentored teachers in the United States, the UK, and the EU. In 2024, she was awarded an Emerging Writer Fellowship from Aspen Words. She is married, has one son, and lives with her husband and dog on Cape Cod.